Trips around the Great Lakes
Volume Two: Lake Huron

David McFadden

The Coach House Press

A Trip around Lake Huron

Toronto

Published with the assistance of the Canada Council
and the Ontario Arts Council.

ISBN 88910-181-7

Other books by David McFadden include:
The Great Canadian Sonnet
(drawn by Greg Curnoe)
A New Romance
A Trip around Lake Erie
I Don't Know
On the Road Again
The Poet's Progress
A Knight in Dried Plums
Intense Pleasure
The Ova Yogas
Poems Worth Knowing
Letters from the Earth to the Earth
The Saladmaker,
The Poem Poem

A Trip Around Lake Huron
is dedicated to Laverne 'Zip' LaFrance —
commercial fisherman, photographer
and member of the Bahai faith —
accidentally drowned
in Lake Huron, January 3, 1979.

I've always felt that selfishness is the deadliest sin. The legendary forbidden fruit is the self. Yet when a writer *tries* to keep out of his writing he finds it impossible. He can go on for years saying this is me, this is not me, and eventually it will all collapse. He'll find his own self in everything. It's something impersonal, at the bottom of everything, creating everything, inventing everything including the illusion of the self-invented personality. His daily attempts to invent his own self, and to keep his own self out of his writing, are seen for what they really are – a tremendous waste of energy.

It's a matter of perspective. Since the eyes through which I see are located in my body, my body seems unrealistically large, larger than the entire Great Lakes. At times it seems somehow larger and more significant than the entire universe. Our lives are small, yet it's impossible to maintain a sense of that smallness for long. People really do become smaller as they travel away from the viewer.

Which is the better attitude for a writer to adopt, providing he has a choice? The one he *knows* to be true yet which leaves him with the feeling he is betraying his senses? Or the one he *sees* to be true yet which leaves him with the feeling of being egocentric? Consciousness of the problem is painful. Yet if the pain is ignored and the consciousness is maintained the pain goes away. For

1

For the Heart Is Continually Breaking

acute pain doesn't last long. And we're left with a sense of vagueness.

This vagueness is not something to be scorned, for the greater the vagueness the greater the need to write with ever greater clarity. For the heart is continually breaking and every breath we draw is a sacrifice.

This is what I wrote in my notebook on the morning of August 4, 1977. I live on the east end of the Mountain in Hamilton, Ontario. The kids were on summer holidays and Joan and I decided to take them with us on a trip around Lake Huron. It was exactly a month after our return from our trip around Lake Erie.

2
Arthur Hailey

In other words I'd rather write like myself than like Leonard Cohen, Shakespeare or Arthur Hailey.

But am I writing like myself?

3
**Fishing for
Salmon in
Lake Ontario**

My next-door neighbour Gene has a heart problem and has had several major operations. Yet he spends all his spare time working on his house – knocking out walls, replacing eavestroughs, painting, laying cement. I tend to do as little as possible in that field. My occupation enables me to work at home in a small basement office.

Because I occasionally receive grants for my work a lot of people around here feel I'm defrauding the government and living off their own hard-earned tax dollars. I get called nasty names, and I've been asked how I can justify taking this money when there are elderly people in Hamilton so poor they are forced to eat dog food. Further, I must be quite clever to have so perfected the art of grantsmanship. Too bad all that cleverness couldn't be put into honest work. Also, I must have been very astute long ago in my choice of friends. The latter remark implies that it must be my well-positioned friends who pull the strings that enable me to get all this money. My pleas that I have no such friends – and that since the money is being offered I am forced to compete for it out of a sense of professional duty – draw only ironic smiles.

These remarks are often directed at me through my wife who finds them kind of upsetting. She wants me to become more commercial in my writing so that we could live off royalties and forget about grants. I'd love to but I can't. Every time I try something stops me. And then again maybe no one can deliberately go commercial. Or maybe everyone is already totally commercial, including me. Maybe I secretly expect this book to sell a million copies. I can see Paul Newman and Joanne Woodward in the movie version.

I mentioned this to Don Bailey who writes movies like *Death Weekend* and episodes for trashy television series like *Kojack*. I described the book, and he said I'd be able to sell it to the movies if I had somebody chasing me around Lake Huron. But I couldn't do that. To me, this series of five books is a fabulous project. In my own world I'm creating something totally beautiful for all time. If I were to add someone chasing me that would destroy everything. So what if I made a million dollars? Would it help me sleep better?

Hamilton. Most of the people on our street are spending their lives working at Stelco, Dofasco, Westinghouse, Procter and Gamble, International Harvester, National Steel Car, and so on. Good factory jobs. In a way I'm seen as a different kind of bird who should have flown away long ago. But I'm tolerated. Sometimes my kids say they wish I had a job in the factory like all the other daddies they know. They don't know how often I wish the same thing.

Every time we drive past a factory, Alison and Jennifer say, 'Oh, look at that. Isn't that beautiful?'

As for Gene, we're becoming fond of each other. He has a hot rod which he takes to the Cayuga Drag Strip, and he's even let me race it along the quarter-mile track. He has a special salmon-fishing boat rigged up and he sometimes takes me fishing in Lake Ontario. He told me that when he was in high school he made friends with this strange artistic kid in his class even though everyone else shunned him. That made me feel good.

One day recently I saw Gene's feet sticking out from under his verandah. He was just repairing the footings but for a moment I thought he'd been murdered and his body only partially hidden. It was a warm day and there was the possible murderess, Gene's wife Audrey, sitting on the lawn chatting with a couple of her friends.

'What's Gene doing?' I innocently asked as I walked over.

'He's working,' she said rather loudly and excitedly. It was as if she had something she'd been hesitant to tell me and the pressure was building up. Perhaps the presence of her friends had given her courage. There was scarcely a pause before she added the coup de grace. *'Some people have to work, you know.'*

So I told Joan. She was livid. 'You just wait till her friends leave,' she said. 'I'm going over there and giving her holy shit. She has no right talking to you like that. There's no one who works harder than you.'

Isn't life wonderful?

When we returned from our trip around Lake Erie we were
shocked to discover our house was full of dead fish. We'd soon
cleared out the fish and buried them in the back yard. Tons of
them. But we still hadn't discovered how the fish got there. And a
trace of the smell still lingered.

In preparation for our trip around Lake Huron Joan and I were
scrubbing the kitchen floor with Boreen Concentrate when Gene
and Audrey came in. It was early evening, a few hours after the
unpleasant incident with Audrey. Joan hadn't got around to
going over and giving Audrey a piece of her mind, although the
thought was appreciated. Actually I'd asked her not to because I
would have been embarrassed.

But this visit was quite friendly. Joan told Audrey we didn't
know where we were going, we were just going. This wasn't unusual for us. Last year we set off for the Agawa Canyon and ended
up in Prince Edward Island. Come to think of it one year we were
heading for Vancouver and wound up in Florida.

Audrey realized she'd been a little too outspoken and had hurt
my feelings. Rather than apologizing she became unusually
friendly in compensation, asking how my work was going and
obvious stuff like that. I had the feeling Gene had told her off
which was also sort of unusual because Gene is usually on the
receiving end of that sort of thing. They stayed on an hour, drank
a few cups of tea, then left. Everything had been resolved. It's not
easy being neighbours, especially when there's a mutual driveway. One can't let things build up.

'Are you sure you don't know where all the dead fish came from?'
I asked just as they were leaving. It was about the twelfth time I'd
asked them.

'I'm positive', said Gene.

'All I can say is you must have an enemy somewhere', said
Audrey.

'Yeah', said Gene, in a serious tone. 'Somebody's trying to tell
you something'.

'Can you still smell it?' I asked, sniffing. They were standing at
the door.

'Oh, it'll be months and months before you get rid of that smell',
said Audrey. 'Why don't you sell your house so Marg and Johnny
can move in?' Marg and Johnny were their closest friends. In fact
Marg was one of the women who were with Audrey on the front
lawn that afternoon when I had my feelings hurt.

I wasn't expecting Joan to get angry but she did. 'Why you

bitch,' she said. 'What do you mean, why don't we move? Lookit, you better get this straight. We're here forever. If you don't like it you should never have moved in. We were here first.'

'Okay, okay, I was only joking,' said Audrey.

'Some joke,' said Joan.

'They think they can say anything they want to me, walk all over me. But they're going to find out that's not so,' Joan said later. She was referring to Audrey and certain other unidentified women. I think she was really angry with me. It just wasn't coming out that way.

That night, the eve of our departure on the second of our five great adventures, I was half-way between waking and sleeping when I heard a beautiful female voice whispering in my mind.

'I am with you always, Dave,' it said.

I sat up in bed. The only woman in the room was Joan, and she was sound asleep.

I could add another commentary here, but the book would end up becoming all bogged down in analysis. Let's get on with the action.

The footings under Gene's verandah had been rotting away and that's what he had been doing, installing new ones. In the morning Joan was wondering aloud about the state of our verandah footings.

5

In the Beginning

'Have you ever thought of checking our verandah footings?' she was saying. 'Has the thought even crossed your mind? People do notice that you don't take much of an interest in this house you know.' She was also a little angry because I'd been playing Othello with the kids instead of helping her get ready for the trip. 'Have you had the van checked over?' she said. 'What about the tires?'

The kids and I got in the van and took the cat to the boarding kennel. When we got back Joan had a pile of stuff at the door ready to be put in the van.

In a few minutes we were off. Our mileage was 59752.8. My watch was broken again and I was fiddling with the car radio, trying to find the exact time for our momentous departure, so that I could enter it in the log book. 'Will you turn that goddamned thing off?' said Joan.

We stopped at a store so Joan could get some books and drawing pads for the kids.

'I don't want to go on this trip,' said Alison while Joan was in the store.

'Mommy's such a grouch,' said Jenny.

'We have to go back. I forgot something', said Joan when she returned to the car. 'I can't be expected to think of everything.' I didn't bother asking what she'd forgotten.

We pulled into the driveway and when Joan got out of the car Bruce jumped after her. The poor little thing didn't know what was going on. He didn't know he was about to be taken all the way around Lake Huron. In fact he had no concept of Lake Huron. To him it was just a-lot-of-water. Joan caught him before he hit the ground and pushed him back in the van. As she did so she caught her sleeve on the door latch, just like that guy in *Rebel without a Cause*. 'Goddamned dog', she said.

When Joan came back Audrey stuck her head out and said, 'That was a short trip.'

'Very funny', said Joan.

'What did you forget?'

'My shorts', said Joan.

'Where are you going? Have you decided yet?'

'All the way around Lake Huron.'

Audrey didn't even blink. 'Have fun', she said.

It was about 6:15 PM when we finally took off. The mileage was 59765.2.

'So it was your shorts you forgot', I said. I was smiling. 'What made you remember them?'

'I saw a girl in shorts.'

I smiled again.

'Do you think you can turn on the charm just like that?' she said, glaring at me sideways.

'God, this is a real reign of terror!'

'Oh shut up!' We drove for a block or two in silence. 'She knows you don't like her you know.'

'Who?'

'Audrey. You hardly speak to her anymore. She can sense something's wrong.'

Silence fell again. We drove for miles in it. It was sort of an inauspicious beginning to what turned out to be a fabulous trip. But before the trip became fabulous the beginning was to become even more inauspicious.

We stayed on Highway 2 all the way through Brantford to Paris. We pretended that the modern superhighways hadn't been built yet. The sides of the two-lane highway were covered with wild yellow snapdragons. I imagined Don Quixote jumping out of his car and tearing them up by the roots because of their fearsome name.

'I just love Paris,' said Joan as we crossed the big bridge over the Grand River and began passing beautiful old nineteenth-century homes with eighty-foot pine trees standing in the front yard. 'Wouldn't this be a lovely place to live?'

We drove slowly through downtown Paris looking for a restaurant. We stopped at a three-storey brick structure with a sign saying ARLINGTON HOTEL / DINING ROOM / COMMERCIAL RATES.

What a nice little family we were, walking across the main street of Paris, Ontario, and into the front door of the Arlington Hotel. We left Bruce in the car. I couldn't remember what commercial rates was supposed to mean.

But there didn't seem to be any dining room in the hotel. Just a bunch of guys drinking beer at ordinary tables, staggering to the toilet, watching television and playing electronic shuffleboard. A tall white-haired old guy was standing there with a silver change-maker fastened to his belt. You could tell he worked there. He might even have been Mr. Arlington.

'Mr. Arlington?' I said. I was the natural spokesman for the entire family.

'No. Mr. Arlington's been dead since 1864.'

'Then maybe you could help me. I was wondering where's the dining room?'

'Dining room? We don't have no dining room.'

'There's a sign outside saying dining room. You can see it for blocks.'

'Oh, are you from out of town?'

'Yes.'

'Well, we used to have a dining room a long time ago but when we closed it up we didn't bother taking down the sign. Everyone in town knows the dining room has been closed down since 1950 anyway.'

'Funny. The sign didn't look that old. In fact it looked pretty new.'

'Where you headin'?'

'Sarnia. That's where we were planning to cross the border into Michigan. We'd decided to drive clockwise around Lake Huron. We'd gone around Lake Erie counter-clockwise after considerable deliberation and we wanted to do something different.'

'Sarnia,' he said. 'Well why don't you stop in Woodstock? There ain't no restaurants in Paris. But Woodstock has some. It ain't far.' **17**

7
Turkey Dinners through the Years

And so we drove on to

WOODSTOCK
THE FRIENDLY CITY
AND DAIRY CAPITAL OF CANADA
WITH EVERYTHING INDUSTRY NEEDS

in the early evening, with young men driving muscle cars back and forth along the main street at fifteen miles an hour, and the light from the setting sun bouncing off the green tile roof of the greystone city hall.

We parked across from the farmer's market and in front of Queen's Restaurant, 'specializing in good food and good service.' Not excellent, just good. A nice Canadian sign.

An old guy in a dirty grey suit and a grey tweed cap and running shoes passed us on the street. He looked as if he knew where he was going. I resisted the temptation to follow him. A pregnant woman walked by. She looked sort of Italian.

The Queen's Restaurant was a lovely old gathering place with mahogany booths and a staircase leading down to the washrooms and furnace room and the big room of cobwebs where they store old cash registers and old Pepsi signs.

There was a bouquet of plastic flowers in a vase on our table. The vase was an old sundae dish with a piece of foam in the bottom to hold the plastic stems. It was a nice restaurant. There were aspidistra and rubber plants – real ones – in the front windows, gold and black velvet embossed wallpaper surrounding the expensive-looking mirrors on the wall, and maroon and gold velvet drapes everywhere. The acoustic tile ceiling was only slightly water-stained.

Sitting behind the cash register, reading a book, was another pregnant woman who also looked Italian or maybe Greek. There was a plaster model of the Venus de Milo standing on a shelf behind her. At the back of the restaurant there were several people sitting in booths. They were sipping Cokes and talking to each other and to the white-smocked waitress who was also sitting there and drinking a Coke.

So the waitress came over and took our order. The kids and I ordered hot turkey sandwiches while Joan's selection was fish and chips. I said I could remember being in a similar restaurant in Dunnville in 1950. It was total recall of my parents buying me a grown-up's turkey dinner – $2.00. I remembered thinking that the potatoes were mashed a little creamier than my mother's. And the gravy was the same colour as the walls. 'It seemed like such a luxurious place', I told the kids. 'I thought I was in heaven. Oh, and I can still taste that turkey. It was delicious.'

'I'm surprised they'd buy you a turkey dinner', said Joan.

I pulled a face. 'There you go again.' Joan has this thing about my parents being a little tight with their money. She didn't know them when they were young and generous.

This is an easy book to write. When I lose control of one story I just move on to the next.

Four guys came in out of the warm night. They were wearing wet bathing suits and bathing caps. Their T-shirts were spotted with dampness from their wet bodies. 'Oh God, it's air-conditioned', said one, shivering.

'Well, well', said Joan, under her breath. 'The local aquatic club.'

I paid the bill. The pregnant woman got up. I couldn't see what she'd been reading. She smiled. I smiled back. 'What are you going to call it?'

I couldn't quite make out her reply. It might have been something like 'Ulysses if it's a boy, Penelope if it's a girl.' I looked puzzled. 'They're old Greek names', she said. 'We are Greek.'

The Woodstock News Depot was next to the restaurant. We walked by. A terribly hunched-up and twisted man came out carrying a bunch of newspapers. 'Don't look at that poor man, Joan', I said. 'There's something horribly the matter with him.'

'Shh. He'll hear you', she said.

Across the street was the beautiful old city hall with its green tile roof. The sun was no longer bouncing off it. It was almost night. Next to the news depot was a store bearing a sign with a picture of a blindfolded woman. The sign over the door simply said BEAUTY SUPPLY. There were some wigs in the window and there were also some rare coins on display. A sign in the window read WOODSTOCK COIN EXCHANGE. Strange combination for a store: beauty supplies and coin exchange. I couldn't figure out why the woman was blindfolded. Another pregnant woman walked by on the sidewalk. She was not blindfolded.

'Everyone in this town', said Joan, 'is either pregnant or Italian.'

'The people who run the restaurant are Greek.'

'You ordered turkey in a Greek restaurant?'

'Yeah. What's the matter with that?'

'Oh Dave. Sometimes I wonder about you.'

On the way out of town we passed Johnston's Jewellers and Art

8
Passing through Woodstock on a Summer Night

Gallery, which was another strange combination. We also passed the Oxford County Museum. 'Oh there's another restaurant,' said Joan. 'It looks a lot nicer.'

'That's the Oxford County Museum,' I said.

'No, next to it,' said Joan.

'Well it's too late now. I'm full. What's it called?'

'It just says RESTAURANT SINCE 1935.'

'It's called the Food-Rite,' said Jenny.

'Hey kids. This is where John Fulham was born.'

'Oh yeah,' said Joan.

'Were Stephanie and Jessica born here too?' said Jenny.

'No. They were born in Southampton.'

Part of me seemed to be floating along beside the van, invisible, listening in. Everything that was being said was profoundly poetic, heavy with the weight of the entire universe.

9

The Smorgasbord of Consciousness

Lake Huron was a rumour of a naked woman lying in the moonlight and we were scurrying towards it like a small party of ants, lightheaded, harmless, full of dreams and sorrows.

There's a certain piece of landscape on the south side of Highway 2 just west of Woodstock that I never pass without feeling a sudden déjà vu. It's merely a house with a hill behind it, a rather long grassy drummond that rises perhaps a hundred feet from the road. It's something about the relative heights of the road and the house and the hill, and the angles of the house and the hill in relation to the direction of the road that inevitably springs a door in my mind. The same trap was sprung by a similar landscape through which I passed years ago while travelling in New Brunswick. In later trips through New Brunswick I could never find that same spot. But strangely enough I think it was just outside Woodstock, New Brunswick, on the New Brunswick Highway 2, while now we were just outside Woodstock, Ontario, on the Ontario Highway 2.

And this time, just a few minutes after sundown, with the sky the colour of the sleeping mind, the landscape had altered. The house had burnt down. The black charred ruins, abandoned, stood there like a grave marker. And still the trap door opened and a chill passed through me.

I call it déjà vu but I don't know if it is because I have nothing to compare it with. Suddenly the landscape becomes mythic with unheard music and as soon as I think about it I'm back on the highway with all the problems of my life staring me in the face: like trying to make sure I'm driving in the proper lane at the proper speed and wondering if the family is going to hold together and if the cut worm forgives the plough.

What has happened? And why can't I experience it more fully? Why does it disappear as soon as I think about it? Why have I occasionally been able to hold my writing up to it and sometimes imitate it yet been unable to hold myself up to it, to let myself be impregnated by its beam? Why for me is it always something that has happened in the past, albeit the immediate past, and never in the present? If it is something that can only happen when part of the mind is asleep why is that part of my mind always asleep when I pass this spot? Is the crucial spot something farther east of this particular landscape, another particular landscape I know nothing about but which serves to anaesthetize that part of my brain by the time I reach this particular landscape which I only mistakenly associate with the experience? And had anyone been killed in the fire? Did this tragedy have anything to do with me?

We continued passing through a series of beautiful Southern Ontario towns and small cities which have been left undisturbed for two decades because the heavily travelled route during that time has been the mighty Macdonald-Cartier Freeway, the famous 401. The towns seemed ghostly, bathed in a silver cloud of consciousness, a fog-like smorgasbord. And every time we slowed down to pass through another town Bruce hopped up to the window, hoping to see other dogs on the street.

By the time we reached London it was night. The Forest City was humming with traffic. There'd been some rain and the streets were a little slimey. A cyclist wheeled through a stop sign and I had to slam on my brakes. Joan cursed under her breath. She was still a little angry. It hadn't been one of her better days. I decided to make a joke.

'Shall we camp in the Andrews' back yard?'

Joan's face went cold. 'I don't think they'd appreciate us dropping in at ten o'clock.'

'I know. I was only fooling.'

'Beulah just isn't the type.'

A few months earlier, in April, Jennifer and I took the train to London. Irene picked us up at the station. 'What do you want for dinner, Jennifer?' she said.

'I won't know until I look in your fridge and see what you've got.'

Irene and I exchanged amused glances although I was a little more embarrassed than amused.

'I was planning to stop off at the supermarket on the way home,'

10

Marks of Weakness, Marks of Woe

said Irene. 'So you can have anything you want.'

'Anything?'

'Yes, my dear. Anything.'

'Can we have hamburgers?'

After Jennifer finished off three hamburgers she started into dessert. 'Would you like another chocolate cake and ice cream?' said Irene after Jennifer had finished her third helping.

'Not right now,' said Jennifer. 'I'll have it at bedtime.'

I had to give a public reading at the Forest City Gallery that night. There were maybe forty people in attendance, but none I recognized. There was no one there I knew would be really familiar with my work. Christopher Dewdney was in Trinidad, Bob Fones was in Toronto, Greg Curnoe was in Vancouver, Russell Seaworthy was in France, and Danny Andrews was in the Arctic. So the atmosphere was a little on the deadly side. But there was Jennifer, in the front row, nine years old, staring at me with such devotion and intensity.

Jenny seemed to know something one wouldn't expect her to know at that age. At least I could see this knowledge in her eyes. She knew that someday she would be all grown up and I would be either dead or close to it. It was as if she knew that the time would come when she would treasure the memory of her father as he was, and she was trying to photograph with her mind every nuance, every detail of the moment. So I mumbled something about this being such an intelligent-looking group I would read my longest and most boring poem, *The Poet's Progress*. It was the first time I'd read it in public. Jennifer's eyes were like black holes into the future. I could feel my heart pumping as I went into my reader's trance. She was the most beautiful mushroom in the forest.

'That was good, Daddy,' she said later.

'Thank you, Jenny,' I said. I had a feeling she had it all stored away in her cortex forever. And if it turns out that this was nothing but vanity on my part, I don't care.

And so there we were driving at a snail's pace through the slimey streets of London four months later.

'This city looks like Hamilton,' said Alison.

It's not really as interesting a city as Hamilton but it's in a healthier state. Decay hasn't set in as badly, nor has cancerous growth. The air is cleaner. And there's something more middle-class about London, both in the look of the residential areas and the people you see walking along the sidewalks of the commercial areas. Everyone looks so ordinary. You don't see as many grossly obese people, or people with horribly disfiguring marks on their faces, or so many people bearing marks of weakness, marks of woe. It's a far less interesting city. Says Russell Seaworthy: 'Hamilton is one big recessive gene pool.'

11
The Man in the White Hat

We were heading west towards Sarnia along Highway 22. It was getting late and Joan wanted to know how close we were to the Pinery Provincial Park where we'd been camping the summer before. I told her it was about an hour away.

'Oh, that's too far.'

I stopped at a roadside country store, bought some soap and a can of dog food and asked the Serbian woman at the cash register directions to the nearest campsite. She rattled off the directions to about three different spots. She apparently got asked that question a lot. We chose the nearest, about five miles away.

The entrance to the campsite was closed for the night but I opened the gate and drove through. I flashed my flashlight over the giant map painted on a billboard. I tried to figure out where to go. There was no moon and no wind. It was mysterious. We finally camped in the middle of a grassy field surrounded by birch trees. There were quite a few small lakes around. There weren't very many campers.

I filled the kettle for tea and plugged in the cord. Joan began making fun of my new white hat. 'It makes you look old,' she said. I'd worn it when we visited her parents a few days before. 'My mother told me you don't look like a kid anymore. Dave doesn't look like a kid anymore. That's what she said.'

12
St. Mushroom of the Cross

We were in the Coldstream Conservation Area which is part of the St. Clair Region Conservation Authority. We were forty-six miles from Sarnia. This information was provided by two teenage girls who were cleaning out the men's washrooms. It was morning and I wanted to take a shower. They just wanted to talk.

'I'd like to take a shower now,' I said.

'Go ahead. We're not stopping you.' They were high-school students working for the summer. Their green pick-up truck was parked outside.

There was no door on the shower but it faced the far wall and they couldn't see me from where they were standing. So I took off my clothes and turned on the water. But they moved around and started mopping the floor in front of the shower, copping looks at me and smiling, trying not to giggle. There wasn't much I could do so I just smiled back and acted natural. If I'd acted shy and tried to cover myself I would probably have become more provocative and more in danger of getting indecently assaulted. They were fairly big girls.

My strategy worked. The girls quickly became bored and left.

It was still early when I got back to the campsite, my hair drying in the sun. Joan was making a huge breakfast of pancakes and fried eggs. The kids went looking for mushrooms and came back with a bronze cross they found on the path. It was beautiful, about three inches long and two inches wide, with a small hole for putting a string through.

13
A Summer Storm

It was a lovely morning but it was marred by one of those emotional flare-ups that occur in the nuclear family from time to time, the sort of thing that seems horrendous at the time but soon becomes a source of amusement in recollection.

We'd been driving about ten miles when Joan put her head on my lap and dozed off. The kids started making a lot of noise in the back seat. I wanted to get them to shut up so they wouldn't disturb Joan but I didn't want to disturb Joan either. So I merely picked up Joan's hairbrush from the dashboard and tossed it over my head in the general direction of the kids, hoping to get their attention so I could motion to them to pipe down. Unfortunately it hit Jennifer in the eye fairly hard. She burst into tears.

Joan woke up and started yelling. She wanted to turn around and go home. Nothing I could say made any difference, so finally I turned the van around and started heading back towards London. This made Joan all the more angry and she started calling me names. Maybe I was smiling a bit. Maybe it was just something chemical between us. But she ordered me to pull over and let her out. She wasn't going to ride another minute with me.

So I pulled up a side road and stopped in front of a bunch of guys sitting beside their motorcycles. They were drinking beer and wearing black T-shirts and black leather vests. They looked as if they'd consider Evil Knievel a sissy. They were looking straight at us.

'I don't want to get out here.' Joan spoke through the side of her mouth. She tried to look calm. She was even trying to smile. 'Move on, will you?' she whispered out of the corner of her mouth.

So I drove further down the road. I hate to sound like a Zen master but I really couldn't help smiling again, and this time Joan really became excited. She said she resented not knowing the bank balance, she resented not being told when money comes

in and she resented me not having a job like normal men. There were other things too. She was throwing the book at me. It was a veritable litany of domestic agony.

And everything she said had a solid point to it.

She said she wanted me to drive her home, she wanted me to let her out of the van so she could go home on the bus, and she wanted me to get out and go home on the bus so she could take the kids around Lake Huron herself. All three.

I didn't know what to do, so I did nothing. That is, I just kept doing what I'd been doing before the storm broke. I drove back to the highway and started heading towards Sarnia. By the time we were in the suburbs of Sarnia the storm had passed, and Joan was smiling.

I checked Jennifer's eye. There was a small bruise but it seemed okay. 'I'm sorry, Daddy', she said.

14
The Day-Spring
by Orlo Miller

A year earlier we took a trip from Point Pelee to Tobermory. We went the long way, along Lake Erie to Windsor and around Lake St. Clair to Sarnia. Then we followed the shore of Lake Huron to Tobermory at the tip of the Bruce Peninsula after which our dog is named.

We got lost in Sarnia on that trip. At one point we were parked at the side of the road in Point Edward, a Sarnia suburb, and were trying to get directions from passersby. I noticed we were parked in front of a church, a small white clapboard structure. There was a sign out front saying that the Rev. Orlo Miller was the pastor. That was a coincidence of the first order because only a week before I'd finished reading a book by Orlo Miller, *The Day-Spring,* all about pre-Colombian European influences on the Americas. For some reason I thought Miller was a bank clerk in Winnipeg. I had no idea he was a minister in Point Edward. This is true.

On that trip we spent quite a long time driving along the streets of Sarnia, talking about the oil refineries and the high average wage and all that stuff. It was a beautiful day, the sun was shining, the flowers were blooming, and I developed some affection for the place.

So on this trip, as we approached Sarnia once again, I innocently asked Joan and the kids if they remembered being in Sarnia the year before. They said no. I couldn't believe it. Only after I filled them in on the context of our visit to Sarnia did they begin to remember it. Maybe next year they wouldn't be able to remember having taken a trip around Lake Huron. But they'll have this book to remind them!

15
On the Road to Hollywood

And suddenly there we were up in the clouds on the Blue Water Bridge joining Sarnia, Ontario, and Port Huron, Michigan. Really, though, there were no clouds. We were up where the clouds would be if there were any clouds. The sky was as blue as Alison's eyes. A reversal of sorts.

Looking down you could see the entire southern belly of Lake Huron as it narrows into the St. Clair River just as it looks on the map. You could tell the map was accurate and it gave you a feeling of faith in man's knowledge. Hey, you know the way Lake Huron looks on the map? Well, we were up in an airplane and it really does look like that.

Only one thing. You couldn't see the names of the cities and you couldn't see the dotted line separating Canada from the United States.

The U.S. customs official was pretty casual. He didn't ask for Bruce's vaccination papers and he didn't ask if we had any oranges. I felt like complaining. Hey, this guy didn't ask if we had any oranges. Where's your respect for tradition?

'Where ya born?' the guy said.

'Canada.'

'Where ya headin'?'

'Down to Hollywood to become movie stars.'

'Okay. Go ahead.'

16
The View from the Back Yard

As soon as we got through customs which didn't take very long we drove into Port Huron, Michigan, and headed for the Lake Huron shore. We were suddenly very anxious to see Lake Huron, a lake we were both familiar with from childhood, from the other side. Even with the bridge hovering above us, it seemed strange, as if we were on the dark side of the moon. The other side of Lake Erie had somehow seemed more plausible than the other side of Lake Huron. It was like looking at yourself from above or behind.

But it was Lake Huron all right. You could just feel its symmetry as it grew wider and wider the further north you went. There was something clear and graceful about the atmosphere of this lake. The horrors of the twentieth century really hadn't penetrated its consciousness. It couldn't be anything else but Lake Huron but it was backwards. It was like when you're a child and you're playing in the back yard. You look up and suddenly realize you're looking at the back of your house for the first time. You know what it looks like from the front but you've never been conscious of seeing it from this angle before.

The U.S. 25 follows the Lake Huron shore all the way from Port Huron north to Point Aux Barques then, still following the shore, it arcs south to Bay City at the end of Saginaw Bay. This graceful loop is familiar to all who love maps. Without the thumb-shaped arm of Saginaw Bay jutting in from Lake Huron, Lake Huron would be all wrong. Georgian Bay on the other side of the lake would have been untenable.

We drove north on the U.S. 25 through towns like Lakeport, Lexington, Port Sanilac (which sounds like something spelt backwards), Richmondville, Forestville, White Rock, and Harbor Beach — all blessed by being on the shore of this beautiful lake even if it is on the wrong shore. The towns and the countryside were uninspiring, unstimulating. Basically there was a back yard sense to it all. There was all of the drabness and none of the sudden beauty that comes with a similar drive along the Canadian shore of this lake. There was an emptiness.

It was summer resort country even this far south however. The spaces between the towns were studded with cottages owned by rich people from the Detroit area. There were tennis courts, marinas, little rows of cottages for rent all the same colour. There were signs like House on the Knoll, COOKIES ACRE, *Wally Girarel*, TOUZEAU RAMBAUM, Laze Daze, and *Snay Road*.

Joan decided to lie down in the back seat and the kids came up front with me. We passed a dead skunk and a field of fresh sheep manure at the same time. What a formidable coincidence!

'Did you fart, Jenny?' I said.

'No.'

'Did you fart, Alison?'

'No.'

'Then it must have been Mommy.' The kids looked back at her. She continued sleeping, a group of little zeds floating above her head.

We passed quite a few rural mail boxes with yellow TIMES-HERALD signs. Then we passed a mail box with the name GRIMES painted on it.

'Grimes rhymes with Times,' said Jenny. I laughed. She looked at me. 'I'm funny aren't I Daddy?'

Outside the town of Harbor Beach there was an enormous sign outlining the highlights of the life of Governor Frank Murphy who was born there. We drove down to the City Waterworks Park on the lakeshore. They had just decided to turn the area in front of the waterworks into a public beach and picnic area with canopies, **27** picnic benches, swings, slides, teeter totters (also known as see-saws), and huge horse chestnut trees. We drove right onto the beach and scared away all the gulls except one who was sitting on the back of a giant turtle who was sunning on a rock about twenty feet offshore. About a hundred feet offshore there was a long cement breakwater and a long low Great Lakes steamer was barely noticeable on the hazy horizon.

There were a couple of other families picnicking in the small park. Some boys were swimming lazily out to the breakwater. Some children from one of the other families were sitting on the swings. They were calling for me to come and push them. That seemed kind of strange. Why didn't they call on their own father? He was just standing there cooking hotdogs on his portable bar-becue, a beer in one hand, a fork in the other, and a cigar in his mouth.

I would have gone over to push them but I had to go to the toilet. It was killing me. There was a little wooden outhouse attached to the old stone waterworks building. But there was no toilet paper. There was no one in the waterworks building but in a smaller stone building that led down into an underground generating room a guy was painting a large turbine.

'Excuse me,' I called down. 'There's no toilet paper in the wash-room.'

The guy stopped painting. He looked up at me incredulously. 'You don't say!'

'I was thinking of using the women's washroom and I was won-dering if you could sort of watch out for me.'

'Are you feeling all right?'

I just looked at him. I had the feeling I was being too polite somehow. It was unsettling. I think if I'd started shouting he'd have been more at ease with the situation and perhaps would have been more eager to help.

He held his brush up so it wouldn't drip paint. The paint was red. 'Don't go in the women's washroom,' he said in a threatening tone. 'There's no toilet paper in there either.' He went back to spreading on the paint.

'Perhaps I could use the toilet inside the large building?'

'You stay outta there, you hear?'

I thought of going to the washroom anyway and using soap and water. But there were no paper towels and no soap. It was a nice clean washroom though. Actually the guy seemed fairly calm. He was as angry as he was likely to get. He would have been nastier if I'd been black. But he knew that an ordinary white man could complain and get him in trouble. They'd listen to me.

'What should I do?' I said.

The guy kept painting for a few strokes, thinking about my question.

'Oh, I'm getting awful cramps', I said.

He sighed and put his brush down. He stood up and began climbing up the winding staircase to ground level. 'You wait right there', he said. I had a feeling he admired my persistence at the same time that he was critical of me for having been caught short.

He went into the large building and came out immediately with a nice roll of pink toilet paper. He tore off a piece and handed it to me. 'I'll wait for you', he said. His face was blank. No amusement, no anger.

It was a fairly generous piece of toilet paper. Almost two feet long. When I came out he was still standing there with the same look on his face. 'Thank you very much', I said.

'You should always carry a box of Kleenex in your car', he said. Of course. That's what I was doing wrong. That would solve all my problems.

'Say, that's a good idea', I said. 'I'm going to do that from now on.'

He smiled a little. The guy's a clown, he seemed to be thinking. Why didn't I realize that before?

18
William Blake

When I got back to the van Joan had the stove on and was cooking hot dogs. I had a handful of *Marismius oreades* I'd found growing in a fairy ring in the grass. I tossed them in the pan. They were delicious. The stems were particularly meaty and they absorbed the flavour of the hot dogs. They tasted like bacon.

And we were back on the road again. I was thinking of how the motor age had shrunk Lake Huron so much and yet it still seemed large. How incredibly huge it must have seemed to the indigenous people of the area – without cars, without maps, without even horses. The world must have been magically endless. No wonder they heard voices. Their lives must have been one long déjà vu. Imagine having a déjà vu without having to think about it immediately and see it vanish like a peripheral fairy! What is happening to us and where are we heading? Even with the unprecedented amount of literature and other cultural artifacts we're leaving behind, future civilizations may find themselves totally unable to get at our minds. We can't really know if we're leaving them what they want because we can't imagine what they will be like. We will be as enigmatic as the builders of Stonehenge, as enigmatic as the Australian aborigine with his dream time and his ability to stand on one leg for days. Maybe more so.

And so we passed through the little town of Port Hope and Joan said, 'What a coincidence! I was just going to say this town reminded me of Port Hope, Ontario, and I saw a sign saying Port Hope.' Neither of us felt the need to rationalize this coincidence by assuming Joan had subliminally detected a Port Hope sign earlier which triggered the thought that the town resembled the other Port Hope. We were quite comfortable under our intimate blanket of darkness. In fact we'd be comfortable in a culture that rejected the notion of significant coincidence. I liked the example of William Blake, who was totally backward in his ordinary daily life. He would personally deliver handbills all over town for his latest sale of pictures. Then he and Elizabeth would sit there all day waiting for people to show up but no one ever came. Someone showed King George III some of Blake's poems and the King said, 'Take them away, take them away!' Yet Blake lived a long life and died with a smile on his face.

19

Even Jane Fonda Isn't as Cute as She Used to Be

For those who see significance in the insignificant – omens in entrails and chance occurrences – it should be recorded that the ST – short for saint – had fallen off the post office sign in Port Hope so that it read US PO OFFICE. Just as we passed the sign the speedometer turned over to 60,000. 'That's a good sign,' said Joan. I don't know if she meant the post office sign was a good sign or the speedometer turning over was a good sign or that it was a good omen for the long life of the car that the speedometer turned over to 60,000 in Port *Hope*. Or maybe that the speedometer turned over as we passed the sign with the ST missing.

We made the northern loop around the heel of Saginaw Bay and when we started heading southwest towards Bay City we ran into a wall of rain. The sky had been churning grey and black for miles. There was a K-Mart in a shopping centre just outside of Bay City and Joan suggested we run in and buy everything we could get our hands on. It was really raining hard. I dropped Joan and the kids at the main entrance then went looking for a parking spot. The dog hadn't been let out to pee for quite a while so both of us got wet. Then I had to run back to the K-Mart. When I got there no one was waiting for me at the door. How inconsiderate! It took me an hour to find them. And when I did find them I was still wet.

'You could have waited for me or asked one of the kids to wait for me,' I said, pouting. Joan was still a little angry from that unfortunate incident with the hairbrush on the road to Sarnia just a few hours earlier. Her anger flared up again, triggered by mine.

I forget her exact words but it was something like this: 'How dare you be mad at me when I have a thousand times more reasons to be mad at you? I've forgiven you for crimes a thousand times as bad as the triviality that has currently aroused your ire.' That sort of thing. So we decided we'd meet in an hour in the Captain Andy Seafood Restaurant.

There were about four interesting-looking mushroom guides in the bookstore and I spent most of my hour comparing them before narrowing them down to two. I finally chose the British book over the American one because the watercolours in the British one were so beautiful. I later regretted it because it didn't relate to the Canadian varieties quite as well. Useless beauty fades quickly.

The only Canadian book in the store was the RCAF exercise manual. The poetry section was worse than in most comparable Canadian bookstores. There were stacks of Hugh Prather books – *I Touch the Earth and the Earth Touches Me* and *You Just Swallowed My Soul!* And then there was a book called *How to Survive in the Suburbs When Your Heart Is in the Himalayas.* I flipped it open. There was a picture of a woman facing a pile of dirty dishes. The caption read: 'Even Jane Fonda isn't as cute as she used to be.' I closed the book and put it down.

Jane Fonda. Hm! For a moment I wondered what Jane Fonda was doing right at that moment. And suddenly I felt as if I'd made contact. My heart turned into a crystal ball and I could see her. She was somewhere in Southern California watching a re-run of *South Pacific* on television.

It was nice to think that this was the same country that Jane Fonda lived in. There was a guy who looked like the poet Ed Dorn standing next to me. He was reading a book called *Forbidden Cures.*

I'd just finished getting the van ready for sleeping. We were in the Bay City State Park. It was raining bobcats and Labrador retrievers.

'I don't really like camping, Dave,' said Joan. She was in a good mood again despite the rain and all. 'I don't like flies in my tea. I don't like being wet and miserable. And when I do camp I like to be able to get up in the middle of the night and pee in the fields. But I won't be able to tonight with all these Jesus big Winnebagos around.'

We were in a canyon formed by a circle of these $100,000 monsters with air conditioners humming and televisions glowing

20
What Joan Would Like Next

away like electronic meatgrinders. They looked as if they might have retractable machine-gun nests on their roofs. And radar to detect people peeing in the fields or making love behind the trees. This was camping?

There was a sign at the entrance to the Bay City State Park reading NO TENTS ALLOWED IN CAMPSITE. True. Imagine! No tents allowed in campsite! This of course was something to do with the average middle-class American family's dislike of adolescence. The ban was designed to discourage teenagers who usually can't afford $100,000 Winnebagos. They can only afford Toyotas with pup tents on the roof. I know a guy who quit camping because wherever he went he found himself surrounded by rowdy teenagers making love behind trees and stuff like that. 'They ruin it for ya', he said. So there you go.

'I know, Joan', I said. 'I was stupid for buying this goddamned van. I just thought it would be good for the family. But we'll sell it as soon as we get back'. Actually I wanted to sell it because I was afraid we wouldn't be able to afford to keep it running. The repairs were incredible. It was rape every time I took it in for repairs. It was our only car so it was doubling as a family car and all. It was costing about $200 a month just to keep it in running order. I should have known better than to buy a car invented by the goddamned Nazis.

Joan was conciliatory in the extreme. 'But you want to go around all of the Great Lakes. This is only number two'.

'That's okay. I'm not going to be childish about it. We'll buy a nice sensible little American compact and stay at motels all the way around'.

Something I said must have put Joan in a better mood. The kids climbed into the van and Joan started joking with them. 'Now kids', she said. 'Isn't this more fun than being in a motel with clean dry sheets and elbow room and a big bathtub and TV?'

Alison looked surprised. She hadn't been in a motel for a couple of years. 'They don't have TVs in motels do they?'

'Sure they do. Nice big colour TVs'.

'Oh yeah, I forgot'.

'And do you know what I'd like to have next?' Joan had a dreamy look on her face.

'What?' said everybody.

'I'd like to get one of those trucks with the camper cap on top of it. No, you know what I'd like to have?'

'What?' said everybody.

'I'd like to keep the camper but just add a nice big trailer so we'd have lots of room'.

32

I can't remember why I was standing in the rain in front of the women's washroom with Bruce in the Bay City State Park in Michigan at eleven o'clock on a summer night in 1977. But I was. I was wondering about my sad life. When I was fifteen my big hero was William Burroughs and I wanted to grow up to be just like him. I was wondering where I went wrong when a black woman in her early fifties came out with a mop and pail and looked at Bruce.

'Oh, look at the lovely little pussycat', she said.

'That's no pussycat', I said. 'That's a full-blooded dog'.

'Really? What kinda dog?'

'That's a West Highland White Terrier'.

'A what?'

'A Westie'.

'Oh'. She had blonde spots in her black Afro hair. 'I had a little dog a little bigger than him about this high. His name was Didhebitecha'.

'Didhebitecha?'

'Yeah'.

'And did you bite him back?'

Her joke had backfired. She laughed. 'Then one day somebody lifted him'. She looked sad. Bruce kept wagging his tail. 'So someone we knew had a friend in 'Troit who had a dog they wanted to git rid of. So my son-in-law drove me down and we got him. He was a lovely dog'.

'What did you call him?'

'Didhebitecha'.

'Didhebitecha II?'

'No, he never bit me. Neither did the first one'. The conversation was getting interesting. 'One day I called him from across the road and he ran out in front of a car and got hit. He was a lovely dog. He never shed. It used to cost me fifteen dollars to get his hair cut. In fact I got his hair cut the day before he got hit'.

'Did you get your fifteen dollars back?' I guess that was a stupid question, making fun of someone whose dog died. But I was getting soaked. So was the woman. She didn't seem to mind though. And I was flattered that a black woman was talking to me, a white man.

'No', she said. 'No refunds on that'. The hair-cut, that is.

She said she had six grandchildren and told me the ages and said she'd lived in Bay City since 1969.

'Where are you from originally?'

'Birmenam', she said. 'Birmenam, Al'bama.'

'Birmingham?'

'That's right. Birmenam.'

'What do you like best, the north or the south?'

'I like the north fine but there's somethin' about home.'

'Yeah', I said.

She said she was going to get a Westie the next time she needed a dog.

'What are you going to call him? Didhebitecha III?'

'Maybe', she said.

I told her about my Uncle Bill who calls his dog Askim. 'When people say to him what do you call your dog he says Askim. So if they're not too bright they ask him. They get down on their hands and knees and look the dog in the face and say, "What's your name, dog?"'

She liked that story. 'Oh that's good', she said. 'I think I'll call him Askim.'

I asked her what her name was. 'Debbie Dobyne', she said. She even spelled the last name for me.

'What's it really like for you living up here in Bay City?' I said.

'It's really a nice place', she said. 'It really is. But they's a lot of snobs.'

22
Tortured with Razors, Burnt with Cigarettes

Standing next to us was a Winnebago with Florida licence plates. The air conditioner was going full blast even though the night was cold and rainy. I dreamt I was back in Ontario in the nineteenth century. For some reason I knew it was 1830. I was in the woods. It was like my old Wacousta dream but this time I had a large trunk that I had to get to Ottawa. There was a narrow macadam road threading through the woods. A bus came along and picked me up. It was the first bus in Ontario. It cost me a dollar-fifty to get to Ottawa. I didn't think it was unusual there would be buses in 1830.

I slipped out of the van at 7:30 and went for a long walk through the woods. There was garbage all over the place. There is a different attitude towards the woods in the United States. Some of this garbage seemed to date back to Civil War days. I could have had a garage sale. There were giant spools of cable, wagon wheels, old cars, bottles, display cases, a stack of old porno books wrapped in plastic, a porcelain and stainless steel soda fountain set.

It started to rain again. When I got back to the van the kids were awake. The guy in the Winnebago came out and switched off his air conditioner. Then it dawned on me that maybe it wasn't an air conditioner. Maybe it was a furnace. The guy looked miserable like most white people in the United States. They always look like they're having a terrible time and can't wait to get home to watch television. They look as if they're just riddled with unnamable and inexpressible fears. As if they just wish someone would shoot them and put them out of their misery. I think if I lived in the US long I'd get a gun and start shooting white people, the really miserable ones. It'd be the nicest thing you could do for lots of them. Debbie Dobyne would understand. They's a lot of snobs.

We drove back through Bay City, past rows and rows of beautiful old homes and churches. We could see the massive First Presbyterian Church across the bay. 'If that's the first I'd love to see the second', said Joan. It was still raining. She said she used to watch a soap opera that was set in Bay City. 'It seemed to be a very wealthy city and it turns out to be true', she said. The show was called 'Another World'. The characters were all successful architects, doctors, businessmen and other wealthy people who could afford servants. Like Debbie Dobyne. 'Oh no, not the doctor', said Joan. 'He didn't have any servants'.

'Why not?'

'I don't know. He just didn't'.

We were retracing our steps a bit because somehow Joan decided we wanted to have breakfast at McDonald's, to go to a McDonald's in its country of origin. McDonald's: getting you ready for the synthetic future. We'd never had breakfast at McDonald's and we were sort of curious. When McDonald's first started serving breakfasts they put a big billboard up on the Mountain in Hamilton, Ontario. It said GOOD MORNING, AMERICA. There were a couple of complaints and the manager of Canadian operations apologized publicly, saying it had been a human error. So they blocked out AMERICA and wrote in CANADA.

Inside they were selling helium balloons for a quarter apiece. The kids didn't want one so I bought one for myself. The proceeds were for muscular dystrophy. I decided to pretend I had muscular dystrophy. I limped to the counter with my face twisted. 'Uh huv muclah dytruhee', I said to the girl. She looked worried. 'Cuh uh huv ah di-coun un muh bruck-fus?' Joan hit me on the shoulder. 'Dave, quit it', she said. 'He's just fooling', she said to the girl. The girl looked sick. She didn't think it was in good taste. Neither did Joan.

The breakfast was really terrible. I'll eat almost anything but I couldn't eat those eggs. I took a bite out of everything and spit it **35** out. Joan couldn't finish hers either. Even the kids thought the food was pretty grim.

There was a copy of the Detroit *Free Press* at our booth. There was a big story on page one about a Detroit business executive whose body had just been found in a downtown rooming house. He'd been tortured with razors and burnt with cigarettes. The exact cause of death hadn't been determined.

23
An Awful Moment in a Woman's Life

Joan refuses to admit she is hooked on shopping. Whenever she goes shopping it's always out of grim necessity. She refuses to admit that she stays awake nights dreaming up grim necessities that will necessitate further shopping trips. But once in a while the truth comes out.

There was a T-Way behind McDonald's. I guess it was like a Zeller's or a Kresge's or a Miracle Mart or something like that. They're all the same.

But it was closed. It wouldn't open for another hour. It was still early, about nine. Joan was trying to hide her disappointment. It became clear to me. She'd wanted to go to McDonald's for breakfast simply because she knew there was a T-Way behind the restaurant.

'I've never been in a T-Way store before,' she said, fighting back the tears.

'That's okay, neither have I,' I said. 'Tell me ..'

'What?'

'Have you ever *heard* of T-Way before?'

'No.' She sounded like a little girl. It was an awful moment in a woman's life. She wanted us to sit there in the car until the store opened.

'Joan, we'll probably see another further down the road.' I was trying to be gentle. 'We'd look pretty stupid, a family of Canadians sitting here for an hour waiting for the T-Way to open.'

'You're right,' she said bravely. 'Let's go.'

24
Dedicated to the McFadden Family of Ontario

We were heading north again. We were on the U.S. 13 that runs along the west shore of Saginaw Bay. To our right was the famous Interstate 75 that runs from Sault Ste. Marie, Michigan, to Miami, Florida, an expressway wide enough to be seen clearly from 40,000 feet in the air.

We were approaching the village of Pinconning which I guess had something to do with pine cones. You could see we were getting gradually into the north country. Coniferous trees were becoming more and more prominent.

I know this will be hard to believe but just then, magically, Joan flicked on the radio, got a local station, and we heard our names mentioned.

'This next song is dedicated to the McFadden Family of Ontario,' said the announcer, 'who are at this moment driving north along the U.S. 13. Have fun in Michigan, McFaddens, and get home safely, you hear?'

Joan and I looked at each other.

'How did they know about us?' said one of the kids.

'Well I'll be damned,' said Joan.

'Somebody from home must have phoned them and asked them to say that,' I said. I felt a little shell-shocked.

'But no one at home would have known we'd be here at this particular place at this particular time.'

'That is kind of funny.'

'And how did they know we'd flick on the radio at just that station at just that time?'

'I don't know.'

It was a country song they played for us. The words went something like, 'I know I won't have to die to know what bliss is, I know it whenever I feel your warm and tender kisses.' I started turning the dial to see if we were going to be mentioned on other stations.

'No. Leave on that station,' said Joan. 'They may mention us again.'

But there was no other mention.

'I wonder who it could have been?' said Joan. 'I just don't believe this. It's simply crazy.'

'I guess it's just one of those things,' I said philosophically.

We stopped at a roadside park near Pine River. There was a beautiful woods of pine, birch and maples. The forest floor was soft and spongey with dead leaves and pine needles, cones and dead branches, moss and lichens. A few unbroken Miller's High Life beer bottles lay around on the surface. I shuddered to think of what lay below. Human skeletons, old buses, rifles, abandoned railway tracks.

25
The Screw Turned Around and Hit the Seahorse

Pine River is the point where the U.S. 13 becomes U.S. 23 and starts heading east along the north shore of Saginaw Bay, and the Interstate 75 veers off northwest straight to the Canadian border. There was too much high-speed traffic on the road to let the senses really open up and enjoy this lovely spot. There were no mushrooms around but I found three beautiful bird's eye fungi —

Crepidotus variabilis – growing on a dead birch branch.

Joan was making tea when I got back. 'This tea's undrinkable,' she said.

'It must be the water.' I told her about the fungi. She said she'd like to see them so I went back in the woods, managed to relocate the branch and brought it back. In just that time about three more cars had parked and the picnic area was crawling with people. All the men wore Farah Fawcett T-shirts.

A really noisy family set up at the picnic table nearest us. They were hollering things like: 'If there's anything I hate it's a bread sandwich. Is that all we've got, bread sandwiches? ... guy pulling that great big boat ... all of a sudden the screw turned and hit the seahorse.'

'Joan?' I said.

'Yes?'

'There was a purple scarf attached to one of the trees in the woods. It was right on the edge of the woods, on the far side. You could see it from the farmhouse over there.'

'Do you think it meant something?'

'I don't know.'

26
The House of Hate

We were heading into Tawas City, which Jennifer was going to have a reason to remember forever. I felt something on my face. I looked in the rearview mirror. It was a pimple.

'Look, kids. Remember that chocolate bar I ate yesterday? Now I've got a pimple.' The kids moaned and groaned.

At that moment we passed a house, an ordinary-looking house, with a sign out front saying HOUSE OF HATE.

I saw the sign quite clearly, each letter as distinct as the pimple on your face, and that's what it said: HOUSE OF HATE. I turned to Joan.

'Did you see that sign?'

'What sign?'

'I wonder why that house would be called HOUSE OF HATE?'

'It said HOUSE FOR SALE, you dink. Can't you read?'

27
Bruce Bites Jennifer

Before I had time to respond we heard a fearsome animal growl in the back of the car followed by a scream. Bruce had bitten Jennifer.

Joan rushed back to have a look. 'Oh God,' she said. I pulled over. But suddenly there were cars everywhere and I was unable to stop. 'It's pretty bad,' Joan whispered in my ear.

There was some kind of arts festival in Tawas City and the place was crazy with people. Lake Huron sparkled in the bright sun. We pulled into a parking lot adjacent to what looked like the centre of festivities. Joan was covered with blood. 'I think he's bitten off her nipple', she said. It was one of those moments. Jenny's eyes looked frightened. But she seemed to be more worried about what we were going to do to the dog.

'It's not the dog's fault', said Joan. 'It's our fault for bringing him on this stupid trip. It must be driving him crazy driving driving all day long.'

I looked at Jenny's wounds. I put my arm around her and gently pulled her hand away. Joan handed me a damp cloth. 'Don't hurt, Daddy', said Jenny. I wiped away the blood. The nipple was still there. There were two ugly cuts, bites. They looked like fair size stab wounds.

Joan took the kids to a park bench to rest while I went across the street to the police station to get directions to the hospital. When I got back some people were trying to push the van. I'd been blocking about eight cars.

Traffic was crawling along as in a nightmare where you can't move. We finally got to the stoplight, turned left, and went past the hospital without seeing it. We'd gone about two miles out of town before we realized we'd missed it. We turned around and finally spotted it, a low white building. We left Bruce tied up outside the car.

Jenny held the damp cloth against her chest as we sat in the waiting room. 'I want to go straight home', said Joan. 'What's the fastest way?'

'Probably the way we came', I said. 'But we could take the Interstate 75 and then the 401 and be back by late tonight.'

There was a good cross-section of mildly injured people in the waiting room.

'What's the matter with *you*?' a nurse said to a four-year-old who was holding his head.

'I fell on my Uncle Joe's chair', he said. 'And here comes my Uncle Joe now. Hi, Uncle Joe.'

There were three young women all with foot injuries. Sprained ankles, twisted toes, and so on. They were amused at the coincidence. I told them about the Christmas I cut my hand on an oyster knife and went to the hospital only to find three other guys in the waiting room of the emergency ward all with hands cut while trying to use oyster knives.

28
Strange Coincidences in the Waiting Room

39

Jennifer sat there waiting patiently with a serious look on her face. Joan became interested peripherally in a fifteen-year-old with a badly swollen hand. 'He's *really* emotionally disturbed', she whispered. 'Just look at his eyes. He should be committed.'

The doctor came in with x-rays and told the fellow he had several broken bones in his hand. He said he should have come in when it first happened because the bones were beginning to knit and they'd have to break them over again. And because he'd just had a large meal they wouldn't be able to put him under. They took him away to the bone-crushing room.

I asked his father how the kid broke his hand.

'Fighting. You wouldn't have a cigarette on you would you?' He came over and sat next to me. He was a boyish-looking forty, with long curly blond hair and a strong smell of shaving lotion. I gave him a cigarette and asked him why his son hadn't come to the hospital when it first happened.

'Ah, he's always coming home with a swollen hand from some fight or another. It's nothing new for him. He can't stop getting into fights. He takes after me.'

I backed away a little.

'No, I don't get in fights any more but I sure had my share when I was a kid.'

He told me his son had his best friend down on the ground and kept punching him in the head until he punched once too hard and he could hear bones snapping. At first he thought he'd broken his friend's head but then felt pain signalling it was his hand.

I couldn't figure out why his son would be beating up his best friend so viciously.

'He's got a vicious temper, that kid', said the father. 'His friend just said something he didn't like. He's always getting into fights. He's vicious like his mother. His mother's always flying off the handle. She's in the psychiatric hospital right now getting shock treatments. She's been in for six weeks.'

After a while the kid came back with his arm in a cast. The doctor had told him he'd permanently damaged the knuckle on his left ring finger. Strangely enough his father was *missing* his left ring finger. He held it up to me. It was cut off clean at the hand. 'Believe it or not I lost that finger sneaking into a football game between the Green Bay Packers and the Detroit Lions in September, 1955', he said.

He said he was home on leave from the army and his girl friend gave him some money to go to the game. He went with a friend but half-way there they decided to buy four bottles of cheap wine with their ticket money and then sneak into the game and drink the wine in the stands. It was easy to sneak into football games in those days, he said. He said he used to do it all the time.

'While we were waiting to be served in the liquor store I showed my buddy the six-dollar lighter my girl friend had bought me. He started admiring it and saying he wished he had one like it. Six bucks was a lot of money for a lighter in those days. Well, he had this beautiful signet ring and I told him I'd trade the lighter for the ring. So we traded.

'Then we got back to the stadium and he went over the fence and I went after him. When we got inside he said to me, Hey, your hand's bleeding. I looked and sure enough there was a lot of blood spurting out. I figured I must have cut it on the barbed wire on top of the fence.

'Then he yelled out, Hey lookit, you've lost your finger. I got my eyes to focus properly and I saw this long, long tendon coming out of my hand and dangling down to the ground and there on the end of it was my finger. I guess the ring must have caught on the barbed wire and just yanked my finger off when I dropped down. Honest to God, I didn't feel a thing.

'Then I'll be damned if my doctor wasn't in the stands. He took me to the hospital, put me to sleep, came back and finished watching the game then went back to the hospital and operated on my hand. Then that Christmas my mother bought me a beautiful ring. I said are you crazy? I'll never wear a ring again as long as I live. And I never have.'

He was a little guy with a lopsided face. His mouth and eyes were somewhat out of line and his nose looked as if it had been broken several times. His son was really a good-looking kid though. The father bummed another cigarette off me then the two of them left. 'It was real nice talking to you,' he said.

———————————————————————

A guy named Dr. Swami sewed Jenny up. He had a heart-shaped birthmark between his eyes. It took just two stitches — one for each cut. He said the scars would go away. But by the look of them now, several months later, he should have used more stitches. The scars are raised and welt-like. They look as if they'll never go away. We rub Vitamin E cream on them every day.

I held Jenny's hand and looked into her nutbrown eyes as the needle went in and out. It wasn't the first time. There was the time she fell off her cousin's bicycle. She brought the bicycle home by herself, with her jaw broken in three places and covered in bloody wounds from head to toe. 'Daddy', she said. 'I hurt myself.'

I'll never forget sitting in the waiting room with Joan while Jenny's jaw was being wired up. There was a *National Lampoon* sitting on a table. The cover showed a human hand holding a human eye in its palm. I placed my hand over it so Joan wouldn't see it.

31

A Triple
Blue Moon

Meanwhile, back in Tawas City. 'What happened to her eye?' the nurse said. I looked. It was faintly discoloured.

'That must be where I hit her with the hair brush', I blurted out. 'Right honey?' Jenny nodded.

The nurse was tall and white-haired. 'Was it an accident?' she said. She was smiling. I guess it was her duty to check out possible child-beating cases.

'Half and half', I said.

Pretty soon we were back on the road heading towards Alpena. Joan decided she didn't want to go straight home after all. She wouldn't let me yell at the dog. 'Bruce', I said. He cocked his ears. 'You're a lucky dog. A lot of dogs have been *shot* for less than that.' He cowered in the corner.

'Don't, Dave', said Joan.

We were between Oscoda and Greenbush. Lake Huron was still sparkling like a huge pool of 7-Up on our right. We were on the same latitude as Owen Sound, the base of the Bruce Peninsula. The sky was full of planes. Huge B-52 bombers from the nearby Paul B. Wurtsmith Air Force Base were flying around in circles in a pack. There must have been forty of them. It was the sort of thing you seldom see in Canada. Helicopters kept taking off suddenly from behind trees.

'Other than that how did you enjoy the Tawas City Arts Festival?' I asked Joan.

'I wish we could have seen it', she said. 'Looked like some nice stuff there for sale.'

'Like what?'

'Crafts and stuff.'

'Wanna go back?'

'No thanks.'

'Next year?'

'I don't think so.'

'Never again?'

'Probably not.'

We passed an ice cream place. 'Let's stop at the next ice cream place', said Joan. 'We need a treat.'

The next ice cream place was Jim's Jumbo Cones. Here's what the sign said:

JIM'S JUMBO CONES

CHOCOLATE MILKSHAKES

CHOCOLATE ICE CREAM

BANANA   FUDGE   DOUBLE MINT

SCOTCH NUT   DOUBLE MINT

24 FANTASTIC FLAVORS BY MOODY

We went in. I meant to ask Jim why DOUBLE MINT was listed twice but Jim didn't seem to be there. They had funny flavours like Blue Moon. A young woman standing next to me had a Triple Blue Moon. 'What does that taste like?' I said.

'Have a bite.' She held the cone under my nose so I didn't have much of a choice. I sunk my teeth in and got almost the whole top scoop.

'Ech, it's awful,' I said, pretending I was retching. The kids laughed. I had blue moon all over my moustache. The young woman handed me a serviette. She was laughing too. 'Thanks,' I said. 'I was just kidding. It tastes nice.'

It was a funny little ice cream store. There were a couple having an argument about what flavours to get. 'What are you getting buttered pecan for, you know you don't like that,' the guy was saying to his wife.

'Just mind your own business,' she snapped. 'I'll get what I want.'

When the guy ordered chocolate his wife said, 'Why chocolate? You know you'll end up spilling it on your shirt and I'll never get the stain out.'

'I'm not going to spill it on my shirt. I'm a grown man.'

'You'd never know it sometimes.'

A girl about Alison's age got a black ice cream cone. 'What is that?' I said.

'It's licorice.'

She accidentally touched her bare leg with it. The shock of the cold ice cream on her warm flesh made her jump a little and the ice cream fell out of the cone and landed on the floor in a big black blob.

Outside the ice cream store there was a van exactly like ours, same colour, same model, same year, and with Ontario licence plates. The driver was from Guelph. He too was taking a trip around Lake Huron. He was travelling with his son. The father had an English accent, the son a Canadian. He told me he'd bought the van in June, 1974 – the same time we did. He'd gone **43**

62,000 miles compared with our 60,000. His was in a lot better shape though.

32
Let He Who Is without Sin Shout the Loudest

In provincial parks in Ontario you have all these helpful students who fill you in on the natural history of the area. Sometimes they even have nature walks at night and show films about whooping cranes and black bears.

There's not much of that in the Michigan state parks though. We were getting into the northern part of Michigan, the part that Ernest Hemingway liked to write about when he was young. We told the guy at the entrance to Hoeft State Park, on the shore of Lake Huron just outside Rogers City, that we were interested in mushrooms.

'They're out of season,' he said. He handed us a pamphlet with some pictures of various morels. 'Morels are the only ones I know of that are edible and you can just get them in the spring.' So there you go.

The other campers at Hoeft made us wonder. You could buy a Rolls Royce or two for the money they threw into their huge Winnebagos, and they'd never have to buy another car again as long as they lived. These so-called recreational vehicles are bigger than houses and about as easy to drive.

Sometimes these camping families would go for walks around the campgrounds but they'd only walk on the gravel roads. They wouldn't think of walking in the woods. The women have beautiful hair-dos, high heels, pastel pantsuits in synthetic fabrics, and their faces are caked with makeup, lipstick and eye shadow. They have TVs in their RVs of course, and they carry teddy bears and portable radios when they go for walks. And they always talk loud so you can hear their ordinary conversation three campsites away. 'Pass the salt, please,' they scream at whoever is sitting next to them and you can hear them on the other side of the woods, over the sand dunes by the water, and even out on the loading pier at Rogers City sometimes.

Talking quietly was unamerican. Turncoats, saboteurs, conspirators and Communists talk quietly. If you don't bellow you must be yellow. You must have something to hide. And we don't like that around these parts.

---

44 The McFadden family was sitting at their picnic bench talking quietly. We were worrying about what to do with Bruce.

'Maybe we should send him to a stud farm for West Highland white terriers,' I suggested.

'That's not fair to me,' said Alison. After all, she hadn't been bitten.

'I'll never be happy again as long as I live if you do that,' said Jennifer.

'If he ever bites Jennifer again or anyone else,' said Joan, 'pphht!' She drew her hand across her throat.

It seemed funny that several times he'd nipped at Jennifer, although this was the first time he'd ever drawn blood. 'Daddy,' said Jennifer. 'He nips a lot when he's just playing but he's just playing. It doesn't hurt.'

We were drinking tea. Bruce was sleeping on the grass under the van. We had a nice spot at the edge of the woods. If you walked through the woods you came over a little hill that turns out to be a grassy sand dune and there you are on the beach of Lake Huron.

'I had a little dog named Sniffy when I was a little girl,' said Joan. The kids listened intently. 'One day a kid on the street kicked him. And Sniffy never forgot it. Until the day he died every time that kid came by Sniffy tried to bite him.'

'Did he ever bite him?' said Alison. Good question.

'No. But he was always trying to.'

'I never kicked Bruce or anything like that,' said Jenny.

33
A Family Discussion at the Edge of the Woods

Across from us was one of those Winnebagos. The owner was walking around his campsite swatting flies. Swatting flies out of doors may not make much sense to you, in fact it may seem to you to be the sign of a weak mind, but in Michigan it's almost a national sport of campers.

This guy was wearing a flowery hat, flowery shirt, baggy shorts that came below his knee, short white socks, and black oxfords. His Winnebago was part of a Camper Caravan. The spare tire cover said HAPPY BIRTHDAY AMERICA FROM EUCALYPTUS, KENTUCKY. The guy had a curly beard. He started belting out a song as he continued swatting flies.

'When it's cherry blossom time in New Jersey,' he sang, 'we'll have a peach of a time.'

The guy at the next campsite yelled out, 'You better not sing any more of that one, Les. There's kids about.'

'Oh, I forgot,' said Les. 'The second verse is even worse.' He was so pleased he forgot to swat flies.

34
A Funny Noise like a Flute

The other guy yelled back, 'You're a poet and don't know it but your feet show it, they're long fellows'. It was nice to see people having fun.

Every once in a while Jennifer would slip into the woods by herself. It was only a couple of hours since she'd been bitten. I guess she was still suffering from shock. Why doesn't Bruce like me? She seemed to be mulling the question over.

Suddenly she ran out of the woods. 'I saw a big raccoon', she said. Her eyes were as black as space.

'Did he bite you?' said Alison. She usually isn't that cruel.

'No', said Jennifer, still too innocent to notice sarcasm. 'It didn't see me, I guess. It just stood there really still'.

The next time she came out of the woods she'd seen a brown and white rabbit and a squirrel.

'Did they bite you?' said Alison.

'No. They ran away as soon as they saw me'. She showed me a large red berry. 'Is this a wild radish?' she said. She stood close to me. 'When the raccoon ran away he made a funny noise like a flute'.

'I thought you said he just sat there'.

'He did at first. I was taking little tiny steps up behind him and when I was this close he looked up at me and ran away and he made a funny noise like a flute'.

The two of us went for a walk. We found some fairy clubs. Bright yellow club-shaped fungi that grow about an inch out of the ground. We ate some but Jenny didn't like them. 'Let's leave them for the fairies', she said.

We went running down to the lake. Jenny tripped over an exposed root and fell down the sand dune. There was no one at all on the beach. Far out you could see lakers steaming into Rogers City to pick up loads of limestone.

On the way back Jenny made a little collection of mushrooms and berries. 'I want to be a botanist when I grow up', she said. She asked if I would buy her a wildflower guide book.

35
Unamerican to Pick Mushrooms

On one side of us were three guys in their early twenties. They had a red Chevy van with a large blue tent. I wondered why they were camping in a place like this rather than in some wilderness area.

On the other side were two girls. They had a grey Pinto and two small blue tents. They were reading movie magazines and listening to schmaltzy music on the radio. They were fat and pimply.

They were sunning themselves on blankets and eating potato chips.

Joan and I walked through the woods to the highway. There was a store there. We went in and bought some postcards and sent them to friends at home. One of the cards had a photo of the hospital at Tawas City. We wrote on it: 'Thank heavens for hospitals. We're having a hard time identifying mushrooms around here.' We didn't mention the dog bite of course. It occurred to us we were quite a bit further north than Hamilton, so we wrote on another card: 'How are things down in Canada?' Hilarious.

We bought stamps and asked the guy where the mailbox was. 'It's right here,' he said, holding out his hand.

We handed the cards to him. 'Don't read them, now,' I said.

'I get so many of these I'd never get the chance to read them all,' he said.

I had a little basket full of mushrooms I'd picked in the woods. I was going to take them back to the campsite, take spore prints, and try to identify them. Some of them were quite beautiful. Striking colours. I rested them on the counter. The guy ignored them.

Three hitch-hikers came in and bought a six-pack.

I couldn't understand why everyone was ignoring the mushrooms. They looked so lovely sitting there, just crying to be noticed. I guess it's considered unamerican to pick mushrooms. Out of season, as the conservation officers would say.

I just couldn't understand this park – people sitting around their Winnebagos playing cards, swatting flies, yelling.

'Tomorrow's Sunday and the next day's bloody Monday,' one guy yelled out for no apparent reason.

His wife was sitting right next to him. 'Now you sound like Bobby,' she yelled back at the top of her lungs. Her voice went ringing through the woods. No wonder there were no birds. It's amazing the trees didn't die.

A pack of joggers went by on the gravel road. They were wearing headbands, T-shirts, gym shorts and Adidas running shoes.

Joan wanted to dig up some young pine trees and take them home. 'They look so beautiful, and no one ever walks through the woods here,' she said. 'They don't even jog through.'

I walked up to one of the conservation officers. He was wearing an important-looking blue uniform. I wanted to ask him if he could identify a mushroom I found. It was a *Lactarius deliciosus,*

36
The Difference between a Mushroom and a Toadstool

47

considered edible and choice as you can tell from the name, but I didn't let on I knew. 'Do you know what this is?' I said.

He examined the specimen closely then handed it back to me. 'That's a toadstool', he pronounced, with quiet pride.

'What's the difference between a mushroom and a toadstool?'

He was completely sure of himself. 'You can eat a mushroom but a toadstool is poisonous.' He glanced at his fingernails.

37
The Trees at the Edge of the Woods

The bearded guy in shorts, the one who'd been singing the allegedly lewd song about blossom time in New Jersey, came over to our side to introduce himself to the two girls camping on our right. They were totally bored with him after about thirty seconds and did nothing to encourage him but he went on and on. They sat there listening and he stood there talking. There seemed to be a lot of tension under his words as if he wanted to ask them something but was too shy. Joan and I pretended we weren't listening. But it was pretty hard not to.

'Oh, I've got a wonderful wife', he was saying. He had a florid complexion under his beard. 'Love is so important in life.' I had the notion he was about to tell them that his wife had a bad back and couldn't make love any more, and would they mind if he ...

But no. 'You'll find out when you get older', he said. 'To love someone without any selfish motives is the best thing life has to offer.' Buried in that last line like a hook in a worm was the information that his wife gives him nothing in return for all the love he gives her.

He went on and on with his philosophy of life. He thought he was really roughing it in the northern woods in his $100,000 Winnebago.

'I've been camping ever since my oldest son was born and that was 1952', he said. 'Every weekend my wife picks me up at work and we drive straight to the campgrounds.'

I could read his mind. He desperately wanted the girls to say something, to ask him where he worked, where he lived. But he was out of luck.

'It's what you know about camping that's important', he kept saying over and over.

'If you don't know anything about camping you'll go home miserable', he said. 'If you know about it you'll always have a wonderful time.' Buried in that statement was the information that he knew a lot about camping and would be willing to impart his knowledge to them if only they'd ask.

48   One of the girls started turning the dial on her radio. The other yawned audibly. We had our backs to them. I thought the guy was going to start quoting from the Bible.

'One time I remember it rained three days straight and the porch started to sink in the mud ..'

I couldn't stand it any more. I gathered up some kindling wood and had a fire blazing away in about ninety seconds. The flames lept in the sky and cast fantastic shadows on the trees at the edge of the woods. It was dark. The kids had their pyjamas on.

38
A Beautiful Woman Spurned

Earlier I noticed a stunningly beautiful young woman riding along the gravel paths on her bicycle. As the fire died down Joan and I were getting ready for bed when we noticed the girl had dropped in on the three guys camping on our left. She was something off the cover of *Oui*. Lucky guys.

We got under the covers and listened to their conversation. There was an open screen on the side of the canvas facing them. I thought an electric storm was coming over the horizon but it was just the girl taking flash photos of the guys in the dark.

'I haven't met such funky guys in a long time,' she said.

'Yeah,' said the guys. They didn't seem funky to me. They seemed sort of slow-witted. But who am I? Merely the invisible one, as always.

'Well,' said the girl. 'I'm too tired to walk back to my tent. Why don't I just stay with you guys tonight?'

'Ah, I don't know,' said one of the guys.

'Okay then,' she said, a little hurt. 'I'll walk home. See ya.'

Joan turned in the darkness. 'She's awfully tired, Joan,' I said. 'Should I run after her and tell her she can sleep with us tonight?'

'No thank you.'

'Ah, that's cruel. Come on, Joan.'

'No.'

39
Grapefruit

Sometimes when you've had a Dramatic Insight into the Nature of Things and you try and describe it to others you suddenly realize it was neither dramatic nor insightful at all. You can tell by the look of boredom on your listener's face. But when you're a writer you're free to imagine the look on your reader's face and although I know this won't sound very dramatic at all it struck me as being a Dramatic Insight at the time.

As I was falling asleep the immense futility of all the great emotional crises of our lives hit me right smack in the face. It sort of exploded under my nose like an exploding cream pie. Ah, so that's it! That was my reaction. It's really all so easy. Look how difficult we make it for ourselves.

In a flash I saw that the whole story of the human race was a fairy tale and we were little magic fairies. Three billion of us. We're born and die in a flash, and in that small duration for some inexplicable reason instead of merely enjoying our brief lives we have to take on all the weight of the universe. Each little life thinks it's the centre of the universe and is responsible for everything that happens.

With that realization a weight slipped off my shoulders. In the corresponding vision I could see the world about the size of a grapefruit. It was covered with tiny lights, three billion of them, each one tremendously worried about its place on the skin of things.

40
Vaseline

The washroom was crowded. It was U-shaped with a row of flush toilets, a row of sinks with mirrors, and a row of steaming showers. It was all very luxurious.

All of the showers were in use. I slipped in front of a vacant sink and looked at myself. It was a grey morning and there's something particularly bleak about a men's public washroom on a grey morning in the United States. Everyone was so business-like. No one spoke. Everyone had his own universe in front of him and was hanging on like a lamprey to a pike.

The guy on my right was grey-haired and in his fifties. He had a Velikovsky paperback in his back pocket. I felt guilty for having looked. No one was looking at anyone but himself, in the mirror. This was the United States on a bleak morning.

I remembered the dream I'd had an hour earlier. I was at home typing out a book of poems and Ezra Pound walked in. He picked up my manuscript and started making changes.

When I got back to the van Joan looked sad. 'I'm homesick for Canada,' she said.

'We'll be crossing back into Canada tomorrow,' I said.

She began telling me about a conversation she'd overheard in the women's washroom. 'A woman from one of those Jesus big Winnebagos was in there with a huge case of cosmetics. She was putting Vaseline on her elbows. Why would anyone on a camping trip put Vaseline on her elbows? She was putting it on her eyes too, on her eyelashes, eyelids, ears, throat ..'

'I don't know. Maybe in a few years it'll be unthinkable to wake up in the morning without covering yourself with a coat of grease.

After all, brushing your teeth in the morning is a relatively new invention.'

'And there was another woman there talking to her. She was saying, "Well, it was just a terrible way to find out. It was really shocking. You know the State Troopers won't tell you."

'The woman kept putting on Vaseline. She had a suitcase full of little jars of things. She said, "Well I know, but I didn't feel it was my place to tell you."

'Then the other woman said, "Well I wish she hadn't told me. It was a terrible way to find out." I wish I'd heard the whole conversation. Now I'll never know what they were talking about.'

Joan was eating a fried egg. She likes to eat all the white first until there's nothing left but a fat golden yoke which she scoops up without breaking and pops into her mouth whole.

'It sounds to me,' I said, 'as if they were trying to make a big tragedy out of nothing.' I looked up and there was Jennifer standing on the edge of the woods with a plate in her hand. As I watched she tossed her egg into the woods.

'What did you do that for?' I said.

'I thought the raccoon might be hungry.'

My heart sputtered a little then started beating again.

So Joan and I decided to leave the kids there looking after our stuff while we drove into town to get some gas and just generally be by ourselves for an hour.

41
Time Warp

We pulled into Rogers City where the world's largest limestone quarry was located. Neither of us felt like visiting the quarry. It was too touristy a thing to do, even for us.

The price of gas was increasing rapidly in the U.S. as in Canada. It was marked at 80.0 cents a gallon on this pump. While the guy was filling the tank Joan and I decided to go into a public library that was located behind the station. It seemed to be an odd place for a public library.

Actually it was quite a large library for such a small place. You walked up the stairs then turned to the right. The walls were made of glass and there were glass tables with plants on them. The library was actually on the second and third floors of the building. I'm not sure what was on the first floor. Maybe some offices.

There seemed to be something familiar about the library as if I'd been there before but I knew I hadn't. It was only later I realized that it was similar in structure to a library that has appeared frequently in my dreams through the years.

We didn't have much time to spend in the library. We looked at a display of new books then looked at each other in astonishment. What a hick place Northern Michigan was. All these so-called new books were ten years old. Strange.

When we went back outside I realized, with a sickening feeling in my stomach, that something really strange had happened. The pumps, the front of the building, the street, everything looked newer somehow than it had a few minutes earlier. The trees looked smaller. Everything looked cleaner.

The gas was now marked at 38.9 cents a gallon. Less than half what it had been a few minutes earlier.

'We've gone back in time', I said to Joan.

'I know', she said, calmly.

'We've gone back to 1967. Look at the cars. Look at the licence plates. Even the gas station operator looks ten years younger.'

'Never seen a van like this before', the guy was saying. I was hoping he wouldn't notice the 1977 licence plates.

'It's the new Volkswagen camper', I said. I didn't feel alarmed. Joan seemed okay too. My mind just plodded along as normal. 'I guess you can't get them in the States yet. They're just trying them out in Canada.' I could see he was puzzled. He was thinking to himself 'if it's so new how come it's developing rust spots already?'

I had a feeling we were going to be plugged back into 1977 any moment and it occurred to me we should try to get to a bookstore and buy some first editions. Too bad we weren't in Canada. I didn't know much about American books.

We paid the guy then parked the car and went for a walk. The town had changed incredibly in ten years. Everywhere we looked there were proud buildings from the turn of the century. They hadn't been standing a few minutes earlier. Cheap chain restaurants and muffler shops had lined the main street.

Even the town hall had been torn down. It was a tall Gothic stone structure with a clock. We couldn't find a bookstore. When we got back to the gas station we were back in 1977. The guy looked at us as we got in the van.

'Weren't you people through here before about ten years ago?' he said.

'Yes, we were', I said. 'You must remember the van. You made quite fuss about it at the time.'

'Yes, I certainly did', he said. 'It was the first one I'd seen anything like it, with the pop-top and all. This couldn't be the same one, could it?'

'No. That rusted out so badly we had to get rid of it. And we bought another just like it.'

The funny thing about the whole experience was the change in Joan.

'I like you better now,' I said.

'I liked you better then,' she replied.

On the way back to the campsite Joan began getting nervous and so did I. 'We shouldn't have left the kids there alone,' she said.

When we returned the kids were talking to a couple of campers. A man and his wife.

'Your kids were telling us their life story,' said the woman. She was in her late fifties and beautiful. A thin, elegant looking woman who reminded me a bit of P.K. Page. Not quite that beautiful though. The kids sat there without smiling. They looked kind of subdued as if this couple had been boring them.

The husband was a fat guy with no chin. He wanted to know if we'd visited the world's largest limestone quarry in Rogers City. I felt sort of guilty about admitting we hadn't. What would W.H. Auden or Christopher Dewdney have said?

'We went yesterday,' said the chinless guy. 'We were lucky, real lucky. A quarry employee was up in the lookout with us and explained the whole thing. They have the world's largest shovel there. Eighteen yards. You can drive a car into it and turn it around.'

'A full-sized American car?'

'Yes sir. A Cadillac!'

· They knew we were Canadians and seemed to think we were in Michigan because we prefer camping in the United States to camping in Canada, as if we thought the facilities were better or something. They just naturally assumed that.

They wanted to know if we'd ever been in Huntsville, Ontario. 'It's a nice place,' said the woman. 'We used to camp on the French River but we had some unpleasant experiences with thievery in Canada. So we sold our camping trailer and bought a big Winnebago. We just go to the state parks in Michigan now.'

'Yeah,' I said. 'Canada is full of thieves.'

Joan started laughing. The couple looked a little confused. 'He's just fooling,' said Joan. 'We've been camping in Canada for years and we've never had anything stolen.'

'But you must remember, Joan,' I said. 'We're not Americans.'

'Yes, that's true,' said Joan.

The couple looked confused again.

42

Thievery in Canada

53

43
The Black Killer

Then we got talking to the three young fellers who'd been visited by the beautiful woman the night before. They were from Detroit.

The girl was right. They were funky. You could tell by the way they dressed, the way they talked and the music they listened to that they were hip.

They told me about the Black Killer who lurks in their neighbourhood. They said they were always getting mugged. One had been beaten up at work by black fellow workers. Another said he was playing baseball with some friends when they were attacked by a bunch of blacks swinging baseball bats.

'It's pretty bad where we live,' they said. 'We try to keep our place in shape but the blacks, when the front of their house falls down they move to the back. It makes you kind of prejudiced.'

They wanted to know what we were doing in Michigan so I told them about wanting to go around each of the Great Lakes. They were unusually curious about us, and they thought that was a fabulous idea. So I told them I wanted to write a book about each of the lakes.

'Hey, that's really cool,' they said.

I didn't ask them about the girl. Maybe they were afraid she was going to steal their cocaine.

44
For Those without Sunday Clothes

We stopped at the gatehouse on the way out of P.H. Hoeft State Park. A big shining new Cadillac was parked there with a smiling fat guy in a clerical collar sitting in it. He was a Lutheran minister and he was looking for a family of campers. He had to deliver a message of mercy. Someone had died. I hoped it wasn't someone from Detroit killed by the Black Killer. It was Sunday morning.

'I suppose you're going to church,' he said when he saw us getting ready to leave.

'Not bloody likely,' I said. He just smiled. He said he was conducting a drive-in church service at one o'clock for 'those without Sunday clothes or who have trouble getting in and out of their cars.'

We were back on the U.S. 23 heading northwest, skirting the shore of Lake Huron. At one point we could see four Great Lakes steamers steaming into Rogers City to pick up loads of limestone to deliver to steel mills all around the lakes.

I swerved to avoid hitting a porcupine. Then we passed a dead porcupine. You could tell by the tire tracks that some motorist had deliberately crossed the centre line to hit it. I shuddered to think we were sharing the road with idiots like that.

Alison was being nicer to Jennifer. 'See this ball, Daddy?' she said. 'Jennifer bought it for Bruce with her last fifty cents.'

I got all choked up and asked Jennifer to come up to the front. 'That was very nice of you, Jennifer,' I said. 'But listen. Don't get close to Bruce until we find out what's the matter with him. Okay?'

'Okay, Daddy.'

Joan got the Lutheran minister's drive-in service on the radio. She said she wanted to see if he mentioned us. But it got too boring and we turned it off.

We were driving through virgin forest. Thick pine and birch, no development, just a perfect highway cutting through a section of this continent that has been left as it always was. It was so beautiful I put on our tape of Beethoven's Ninth Symphony as performed by the Berlin Philharmonic conducted by Herbert von Karajan. The last time I'd played it was the summer before as we drove along the glorious Matapedia River in Quebec.

We stopped at the side of the road. It was a Michigan Registered Historic Site. The plaque said: '... Much of the shore is still as wild as when the Huron Indians were the only travelers on this lake.'

We walked along the wave-zoned shore. It was quite dreamy. Huge bleached pieces of driftwood had been left high and dry. The beach was about ten feet wide at this point. Behind it was another ten feet of tall grass and then the highway. On the other side of the highway the forest began. There were no cars on the road. Everything was grey and misty.

And silent. There seemed to be a mystical silence that swept through the four of us as if we had never been born. I'd been reading the Canadian poet Charles Sangster (1822-1893):

> *The feet*
> *Of the Red Man have pressed each wave-zoned shore,*
> *And many an eye of beauty oft did greet*
> *The painted warriors and their birchen fleet,*
> *As they returned with trophies of the slain.*

There were no boats on the lake. Bruce was running free. He took a drink from the lake. We walked for about half a mile and then it started to rain.

Back on the road we passed a sign stating this was the Black Lake State Forest. Occasional large homes had been built on lots cut out of the forest and real estate signs began to proliferate.

One of the homes had a sign out front saying BEER CAN COL-LECTION — BUY, SELL OR TRADE.

46
The Home of Chicago Steaks

Cheboygan is at the top of Michigan's Lower Peninsula, a little southwest of the Straits of Mackinac. If you fly CP Air from Winnipeg to Toronto you fly right over this area.

A large sign on the outskirts of Cheboygan proclaims the town is the Home Port of the Icebreaker Mackinaw. Cheboygan's not much bigger than Rogers City and even though it can't boast the world's largest limestone quarry and the world's largest shovel it's a little better known than Rogers City maybe because Cheboygan is a funnier name than Rogers City.

It's a nice town with a northern feel about it. It's the Yellowknife of the United States. We parked on the main street in front of Wretched's Donut Shop (closed till further notice). We passed Cliff's Live Baits then decided to get something to eat. We went into the Carnation, Home of Chicago Steaks. A sign painted on the window said SINCE 1925 — PICK YOUR OWN STEAKS.

'Do we go in the back to pick our own steaks?'

'Oh, they don't do that anymore,' said the waitress. She said that was discontinued when the restaurant was remodelled years ago.

'You been here that long?'

'Sometimes it feels that way.'

47
If You Seek a Pleasant Peninsula

If you seek a pleasant peninsula ... look about you. That is the official motto of the state of Michigan.

The official bird of the state of Michigan is the robin.

The official gem of the state of Michigan is the Isle Royale greenstone.

The official stone of the state of Michigan is the petoskey.

Michigan even has an official fish. It's the trout.

Its official tree is the white pine.

Its official flower is the apple blossom.

48
Songs of the American Railroad Man

Across from the Carnation was a beautifully maintained old building called the Steffins Block, dated 1904. There were about four ground-floor stores including the Log Mark, a bookstore and news depot, closed for Sunday. There was a little sign on the door at foot level reading KICK GENTLY HERE.

I looked through the window. Prominently displayed was a book called *Cheboygan: From the Heart* by Jim Cohoe.

There was a photocopy machine and rustic pine display of racks and tables. There were several colour portraits by the local photographer Martha Olechowski.

There was a book of photographs of old Detroit called *Yesterday's Detroit* by Frank Angst, and a biography called *Chief Wawatam — The Story of a Hand-Bomber* by Frances D. Burgtorf. *Isle Royale Shipwrecks* by Frederick Stonehouse had a beautiful cover drawing of an old excursion steamer going down in Lake Superior. *Wood Butchers of the North* by Ellis Olson featured a cover illustration of various brands used by loggers. I guess they'd be called log marks and that's probably where the store got its name.

Regionalism was certainly strong in Cheboygan. Also on display were three volumes of *Michigan Ghost Towns of the Upper Peninsula,* and *A Treasury of Railroad Folklore: The Stories, Tall Tales, Traditions, Ballads and Songs of the American Railroad Man* edited by B.A. Botkin and Alvin F. Harlow. I said a little prayer that maybe someday *A Trip around Lake Huron* would be available in the Log Mark.

49

Bliss Carman and the Call of the Wild

Bombing out of Cheboygan we passed a roadside park dedicated 'in honour of the great American poet, Bliss Carman, (1861-1929)'.

So we couldn't resist stopping for a minute. There was a little plaque telling about Bliss and his work but it didn't mention that he was born in Canada and is known in Canada as a Canadian poet. It reminded me of the plaque in Sandusky, Ohio, which contains Col. John McCrae's 'In Flanders Fields' without mentioning that McCrae (1872-1918) was a Canadian and served as a medic with the Canadian Army.

There was a phone booth in the park and the phone was ringing. Since I was standing next to it I decided to answer it even though I was pretty sure it wouldn't be for me.

It was a high-pitched voice: The woman sounded a little drunk.

'This is Reenie. How's your weenie?'

'I beg your pardon?' My first obscene phone call and it was in verse. What would Bliss have thought?

'What are you doin', you silly ol' pervert? Playin' with yer pecker?'

I hung up.

A few miles further on we stopped at the Call of the Wild, a roadside tourist trap. It was a strange-looking building, plaster-sculpted and painted in two tones of brown presumably to resemble a cave or maybe a mountain. There was a stuffed bull moose standing on top of the building and on each side of him was a thirty-foot flagpole, one flying the Stars and Stripes and the other the flag of Michigan.

A woman at the door was taking admission. Two bucks for adults and seventy-five cents for kids. Joan and Alison decided to save their money but Jennifer wanted to see the animals so I gave the woman $2.75.

The woman had a high-pitched voice and was quite merry, as if she had a bottle of gin stashed under the counter. Her name was Irene.

'Do people ever call you Reenie?'

'Sure. That's what everybody calls me. But my real name is Irene. Just like that song. "Everybody calls me Speedoo but my real name is Mr. Earl." She sounded wound up.

'Excuse me for bringing this up, but I just got an obscene phone call and ..'

'An obscene phone call? You?'

'Yeah. What's the matter with that?'

'Nothing at all, believe me.'

'It was at a pay phone at the Bliss Carman Memorial Roadside Park.'

'Far out!'

'And the girl sounded a little like you. In fact she sounded a lot like you. And she said her name was Reenie!'

'It wasn't me, dear. This Reenie ain't into obscene phone calls. Not yet anyway.'

'You want to know what she said?'

'Yeah. Let's hear it.'

'She said, "This is Reenie, how's your weenie?"'

'No. It wasn't me, dear. If I wanted to know how your weenie was I'd just pull it out and look at it.'

50

Actually Experiencing the Call of the Wild

The place was full of stuffed animals. It was grotesque and I felt I shouldn't have brought Jenny in. She was silent and wide-eyed as she looked at a pair of snowy owls, one at rest and one with wings spread as if about to take off, mounted on the tops of dead stumps. Since the snowy owl is seldom found south of the 49th parallel it occurred to me the pair must have been shot north of the border.

The black bear was wired to stand up straight on its hind legs. I wondered what our reaction would be if some time in the future the bears take over the world and put stuffed humans on display.

'That would be awful, Daddy'. Jennifer had such a serious look on her face.

There were speakers all over the place blasting out tapes of owls hooting, wolves howling, bears growling, and so on. There was even a poetry nook where you could buy cheaply printed pamphlets of nature verse.

A beautiful deer specimen was mounted and placed in such a position that it looked as if the front part of its body were running and the hindquarters stationary. Its head was turned straight at the viewer. It was standing in front of a mural depicting a highway cutting through a pine forest. The centre line of the highway continued out on the floor beneath the deer's feet. It looked as if it had been startled by a car and was about to be hit.

'Can we go now, Daddy?'

'Don't you like this place?'

'It gives me the creeps'.

'Okay. Let's go'.

On the way out we noticed a sign saying CALL OF THE WILD IS AIR-CONDITIONED AND COMFORTABLE IN ANY KIND OF WEATHER.

In Kenora, Ontario, there is a stuffed bear dressed up like Santa Claus. It's in the window of a hardware store next to the bus terminal. It's about three feet tall, standing on its hind legs. It's dressed in a red cap, glasses, and a false beard.

———————

51
Hart Crane, Canadian Poet

Mackinaw City looks a little like Banff or Jasper without the mountains. In the summer it's jammed with people who wander aimlessly in and out of restaurants and gift shops and penny arcades. We stopped at Lookout Point under the southern end of the spectacular Mackinac Bridge which spans the Straits of Mackinac where Lake Michigan for the past couple of millennia had been ejaculating its waters into Lake Huron under a solemn New World sky. Once, in Vancouver, an Indian stopped me and asked if I could direct him to the New World. Turned out he meant the New World Hotel on Powell Street.

Because of the problem with the dog we'd already decided not to bother visiting Fort Michilimackinac. It's actually on the Lake Michigan side and we figured it'd be best to leave it until we took our trip around Lake Michigan.

We got out of the car and put quarters into the coin-operated telescope and took turns peering out at the straits and at the lake steamers, yachts, ferry boats, sailboats, barges, and the occasional canoe all passing through and at the cars and trucks streaming across the bridge high overhead.

Then we looked at Mackinac Island where the Canadian poet Hart Crane spent so many summers as a child. The incredible summer homes of rich Americans, the Governor's Mansion, the Grand Hotel with its mile-long porch shimmering in the haze. Of course I know Hart Crane wasn't really a Canadian just as John McCrae and Bliss Carman weren't really Americans. Of course a Canadian, like a Mexican or a Bolivian and so on, is always an American, while an American is very seldom a Canadian.

Mackinac Island from this angle looked more highly developed than the mainland, although cars weren't allowed on the island. Travel was only by foot, horseback and bicycle. To the south of Mackinac was the much larger but less highly developed Bois Blanc Island. The high cliffs of Mackinac Island made me think it was connected somehow with the Niagara Escarpment and it almost certainly is. What we know as the Niagara Escarpment is really just the rim of one side of a saucer-shaped geological depression, the other side cutting through Minnesota. But it's not as noticeable on the U.S. side because there hasn't been the same kind of glacial erosion working away on it.

With its churches, huge hotels, chalets, castles, old houses, mansions, Mackinac Island looked like Quebec City with touches of Monaco. I kept thinking of Hart Crane.

'That bloody Hart Crane never did a day's work in his life.'

'Is he still alive?' Joan thought maybe he would be an old man living alone in a suite of rooms on the top floor of one of those hotels.

'No. He drowned himself. Jumped off a cruise ship in the Caribbean.'

'What did his father do?'

'He was a candy manufacturer. He made Life Savers. In fact he invented them.'

'Life Savers? There you go. He did it to spite his father. His father invented Life Savers but couldn't save his son's life.'

'Yeah.'

We drove over to the ferry landing and got out of the car. It was busy. Ferries for the island were leaving every few minutes, loaded with tourists. I wanted to go over to the island but Joan was worrying.

'Let's not push our luck with the dog. It's really asking a lot of him. What if he bites somebody on the boat?'

'Yeah. He's tasted blood now.'

60   'Tsk. You're being unfair to the dog. He's sick. Look at him shivering. He's just not feeling right. Remember how sick you were when you had your gallbladder operation.'

We decided to postpone our trip to Mackinac Island indefinitely.

'It'll give my readers something to look forward to.'

'Yeah. All twelve of them.'

'But twelve good ones.'

Joan picked up the dog and put him back in the van.

'Look. He's cringing. He's just not feeling well. He's really tired and lagging and it's not even that hot out. We'll board him out next year when we take our trip around Lake Michigan. And we'll not only visit Mackinac Island, we'll stay the night at the Grand Hotel.' Joan was talking big because she was due to start a steady teaching job in September.

'It's a deal,' I said. 'And we'll probably have more money next year.'

'If we're still together.'

52
What We Said While Crossing the World's Largest Suspension Bridge

To be reminded that something is the world's greatest or the world's largest or the world's sweetest or whatever takes away the pleasure of enjoying it. We'd bypassed the world's largest limestone quarry and the world's largest shovel in Rogers City and Bruce's illness prevented us from visiting Mackinac Island and seeing the world's largest summer hotel with the world's longest porch. But we couldn't avoid going over the world's largest suspension bridge which we were doing right now. The Mackinac Bridge. You can see it when you look down from the CP Air flight from Winnipeg to Toronto. It looks like a tiny pencil stroke joining two peninsulae.

Joan felt a little sick. She doesn't like heights. She was worried that a sudden gust of wind from Lake Michigan would blow us off the bridge. She looked to the left and then to the right, cautiously.

'Is that Lake Michigan right there?'

'Yes.'

'And is that Lake Huron right there?'

'Yes.'

'Look, kids. That's Lake Huron and that's Lake Michigan, the world's biggest lake.'

'No. That's Lake Superior.'

Joan misunderstood. 'Oh. I'm sorry, kids.' She pointed at Lake Michigan. 'That's Lake Superior.'

'No, no. That *is* Lake Michigan but Lake Superior is the world's largest lake. Except of course for the Caspian Sea which is really a lake although it's called a sea.'

'Oh'.

'And we'll be catching a glimpse of Lake Superior tomorrow'.

'Oh'.

The bridge seemed to make no impression on the kids. The most incredible feats of twentieth-century technology leave them cold. It's an interesting generation coming up.

53
A Respite from the Ordinary

It seemed as if we should be heading into Canada via this bridge. But no, it just takes you over the Straits of Mackinac to Michigan's Upper Peninsula, a piece of land separating Lake Michigan from Lake Superior. Under the northern end of the bridge was an asphalt parking lot filled with cars, trailers, vans, motorcycles and campmobiles of all sizes. We pulled in and parked but didn't know quite why. Perhaps the others didn't either. Maybe our brain waves were being influenced by some high-frequency broadcasting unit in the United States Tourist Bureau.

There were two buildings set in the middle of the vast parking lot. One was a washroom and the other a tourist office. It was hard to tell them apart. The tourist office was merely a storehouse for hundreds of thousands of flyers advertising various tourist traps in Michigan. The kids picked up flyers advertising the Dutch Village and Windmill Island in Holland, Michigan, and immediately wanted to go.

'No. We can't go there. It's 350 miles out of our way'.

'Awww!'

'Maybe we'll go next year when we're taking our trip around Lake Michigan'.

I looked at the pamphlet. The Dutch Village was advertised as a 'world of pleasure in an "old world" setting', and a 'respite from the ordinary'. You could watch Dutch folk dancers dancing around an old guy in Dutch costume making wooden shoes. You could see windmills, watermills, canals, a Dutch Market, a Dutch Cheese Store, and a Dutch Candy Store.

All this under a tall flagpole flying the Stars and Stripes.

54
As Funny as a Cloud

The place was called the Foot of the Bridge Information Booth. It was strategically located at the intersection of at least two major tourist routes: the route along the eastern shore of Lake Michigan and the route along the western shore of Lake Huron.

When we got back outside there were dozens of people taking pictures of seagulls. There was quite a lot of activity in the parking lot. A lot of people were being pushed in wheelchairs, at least three of the people taking pictures had hare lips, and quite a few people seemed to be walking with a great deal of difficulty. Human tragedy seems to abound at points where two Great Lakes meet.

'It's kind of exciting isn't it Joan?'

'What is?'

'Living through an experience you know you're going to write about later, something you know is going to go into your book.' I guess I sounded a little pretentious, as if I needed deflation. Joan always knows.

'What a pompous ass!' she said.

Alison overheard this last exchange and felt sorry for me. A kneejerk reaction but one I always appreciate.

'Is it going to be a good book, Daddy?'

'Pretty good I think.'

'Funny?'

I couldn't figure out if it was going to be funny or not. Sometimes something that wasn't funny when it was experienced becomes hilariously funny when you tell it. And vice versa. And then there is the unintentional humour of my writing as one particularly perceptive critic pointed out.

'About as funny as those clouds floating over the Mackinac Bridge.'

'Oh.'

'Actually it depends on what happens on the trip. If funny things happen to us the book will be funny. If sad things happen the book will be sad.'

'So far it must be sad then.'

'What do you mean?'

'The fight and Bruce biting Jennifer and all.'

'Yeah. But there have been funny things too.'

'Like what?'

'Like this conversation for instance.'

'Oh Daddy.'

It was still early in the afternoon but Joan wanted to check out an idyllic campground we'd seen from the bridge. It was on the north shore of the Mackinac Straits. A mile east of the bridge. 'Let's just look at it and if we don't like it we'll go on further.'

It was called Mackinac Straits State Park.

'Can you say that, Jennifer?'

'No.'

55

Richard Nixon in Drag

'How about you, Alison?'

'Mackinac States Strait Park?'

'How about you, Joan?'

'Mackinac Strait States Park?'

The guy behind the counter in the gatehouse was proud of his uniform and his role in the Michigan state government service. Wouldn't you be? He was smoking a pipe and looked vaguely Canadian, like Bliss Carman. A big line-up was growing behind us.

'The Michigan state parks are the best in the country,' he said. 'And this is the best of the lot.'

'That's what they said all down the line.' The ambiguity was unintentional. He took it the wrong way.

'Oh,' he said. His feelings seemed hurt.

'No. What I mean is, they said all the way down the line that this was the best park. That's why we came here. Whatever you do, don't miss Straits State park. That's what everyone said.'

The guy seemed to pull himself together after that speech.

'Which way are you travelling?' He knew we were Canadians.

'We came up the Lake Huron shore.'

'Really? Most people come up the Lake Michigan shore. It's a lot nicer. Lots more to see.'

Joan said she wanted a campsite right on the beach.

'That's not possible,' said the guy. 'You have to get here at eight o'clock in the morning to get a spot right on the beach.' The guy was proud of his park. He told us we could look at campsites 84 and 141 and come back and tell him which we wanted.

But 84 was occupied and when we pulled into 141 someone came in behind us.

'Excuse me but we have this spot.' The guy was waving a red token. I looked at it. It had the number 141 on it. He was smoking a pipe too just like the guy in the gatehouse but he wasn't wearing a uniform. Neither was his wife. Neither of them looked Canadian. He looked like Tony Perkins and she looked like Shirley Temple Black. Most Americans look like someone famous.

When we got back to the gatehouse there was a line-up of campers waiting to get in. The tension was as heavy as the sun was hot. The guy behind the counter had let his pipe go cold. I barged to the front of the line.

'Remember me?'

'Ahem! Yes I do.' He was trying to be polite.

'Remember you told me I could look at 84 or 141 and choose one then come back and register?'

64   'Yes?'

'Well 84 was occupied and you subsequently gave 141 to someone else.'

'You looked at 84A.' He took the map out of my hand. 'Eighty-four A is here. Eighty-four is here. There's no one in it.'

When we got back to the real 84 Joan was getting angry. 'I'm not taking this spot. There's no trees and no privacy.'

I think Joan was a little put off by the woman sitting at the next campsite. She was wearing a beehive hairdo and was staring at us with a mean expression on her face. She looked like Richard Nixon in drag.

'Let's get out of here. It's all spoiled. I don't want to camp here. Let's not even stop to get our money back. Let's just go.'

I was willing to take off but I didn't want to lose my four dollars. At the gatehouse the line-up was longer and the tension heavier. Again I barged to the front.

'Eighty-four is not to our liking. Would it be possible to get our money back?'

The guy had loosened his pale yellow government-issue tie. 'No you can't. But here. Take number ten. Someone pulled out just a minute ago. It's right on the lake.'

'I hope it's to my wife's liking.'

'Don't worry. It will be.'

56
Bruce Vomits in My Hat

There were little white sailboats bobbing out on the straits, bobbing among the islands in the stream. Cool breezes were bringing in puffy white clouds of pleasure from Lake Michigan. Cars were going over the Mackinac Bridge like beads of dew along the strand of a cobweb five miles long. The bridge gradually disappeared into the afternoon mist on the south shore.

I knew exactly where we were geographically. We were located precisely at the centre of gravity of the entire Great Lakes system, the point of balance. We were at the centre of the watery universe. Any water anywhere in the entire universe had at one time passed through these straits and was akin to the water that was now passing through these straits, and into Lake Huron just off to the left.

It was as if we had shrunk in size and what had seemed small on the map was really immense. The Great Lakes really comprised an enormous water system, so enormous the imagination is unable to grasp the imensity of it all and can only reduce it for human consumption. It was the sort of immensity only the gods can truly appreciate. But now somehow the human imagination had succeeded. Our concept of the lakes became lifesize and we were the ones to be reduced, and in being reduced we became gods. It was quite poetic really.

There were dozens of pretty girls in bikinis lying on the beach. Above them fat gulls were soaring, content with not being human. Suddenly the girls were naked, lying there without even their bikinis, and the gulls were flying up there wearing little swimsuits and with lipstick on their beaks.

Alison came running down from the public washroom.

'I was in the toilet and this lady was talking to herself. She was saying, "Oh my God, I've got such a headache." Then I flushed the toilet and she looked startled as if she didn't think anyone was there.'

'Was she embarrassed?'

'Yeah, I think so.'

'You shouldn't have flushed the toilet,' I said. 'You should have listened to see how the conversation developed. Maybe she would have started telling herself the story of her life. Like, I was born in Elk Rapids, Michigan, in 1927, and things started going wrong right from the start.'

Joan wasn't amused. 'I don't see what's so funny about that.'

'But then Alison could have told me everything she said and it could have made an interesting story for the book.'

'To hell with your book. That woman probably did have a helluva headache and I feel bad for her. You don't know what's happened to her to make her have the headache.'

'Yes dear.' One of the things about me that has always bugged Joan is my superior attitude. She tolerates me when I make fun of other men, but when I make fun of women she puts her foot down. As for making fun of myself, I don't very often do that except in my writing. In reality I take myself *very* seriously. I really don't know how Joan and the kids stand me. I laugh at other people behind their backs but I never laugh at myself, not even behind my back, and that is about the most despicable stance a human being can take. No one likes a person like that. I like myself though. I think I'm just fine. That's what makes it all the worse.

Anyway I went for a shower. Ah such luxury, it was like the Ritz Carlton Hotel all over again. Canadian parks were never like this. Each shower had its own skylight and there was enough room for me and at least twelve beautiful girls from the beach to shower all at the same time. I left the shower door unlocked hoping that a bunch of them would barge in and join me. After all, it would have made for a socko chapter in the book. But sad to say it didn't happen. Oh God, will my fantasies *ever* be fulfilled?

66   When I got back all clean and cooled off I began digging around in the van looking for my white hat. The sun was too hot for me. When I finally found the hat it was crushed and dirty. There were dogprints all over it. Then I noticed Bruce had puked in it.

While washing the hat out and setting it in the sun to dry I overheard Jennifer having a serious discussion with Bruce.

'Bruce, if you ever bite anybody again we're going to have your teeth taken out. Do you understand? Do you?'

There was something evil about these two boys, brothers, about six and eight or seven and nine years old. Maybe it was their shaven heads, their narrowed eyes, their identical black bathing suits. They seemed to be grinning at me menacingly. One of them had a toy gun in his hand.

I was sitting on a swing in the camp playgrounds. Alison and Jennifer were playing on the teeter totter. Joan had been with us, holding Bruce on his leash, but had wandered off somewhere without saying anything.

The boys kept looking at me. I was a key figure in a threatening world, and they were suspicious. I walked over to them and smiled. Their expressions didn't change.

'Can I have a look at your gun?'

The face of the older boy softened somewhat as he handed me his small black cap pistol. It was made in Spain and had the word *Pirata* marked on it. He told me to look. He pulled a red pellet from a leather pouch I hadn't noticed strapped to his wrist. He took the gun from my hand and placed the pellet behind the cocked hammer. He pulled the trigger.

Bang! It sounded like a starter's pistol. My ears were ringing. The boys looked at me as if I might be fun to kill.

'Want me to shoot you?' said the older.

'No. Not today. Maybe when I'm old and sick you can shoot me.'

'You're pretty old now and you look kinda sick.'

'No. I'm too young to die.'

'I'm gonna shoot you anyway.'

He fired at me.

I died dramatically, going down, holding on to the swing then collapsing on the ground. Lying there, face up, I opened one eye a crack. The kids were still looking at me. The older one was recocking his gun.

'I'll shoot him once more just to make sure he's dead.'

Then I noticed Joan walking across the field with Bruce.

'Do me a favour? See that woman? Shoot her for me.'

The kid fired at Joan. She was genuinely startled. She grabbed

her chest and almost collapsed. Then when she saw it was just a
toy gun she became annoyed.

I noticed two guys in their early thirties had been sitting a few
feet away drinking Miller's High Life beer, listening to country
and western music on their car stereo, and watching me intently.
They hadn't said a word. They just watched silently. They had
Indiana licence plates.

'Did you tell that kid to shoot me?' said Joan.

'It was just a game.'

We left and walked towards the beach.

'Did you see those guys drinking beer?' said Joan. 'They looked
really weird.'

'I know.'

58
Bruce Is Not Himself

The kids threw small pieces of bread into the air and suddenly the
beach was solid with gulls. They came from all over Lake Huron
and all over Lake Michigan. Some were even swooping down
from Lake Superior. Bruce just sat there watching. Joan looked
sad.

'I'm worried about Bruce. Why isn't he chasing the gulls?'

'Maybe he's tired. Maybe he prefers buoys.'

'I think something's wrong with his mouth. Come here, Bruce.'

Bruce ambled over slowly, his tail wagging pitiably. When Joan
tried to pry open his mouth and look inside he wrenched his head
away.

'See? There's definitely something the matter. I think it's from
when Jennifer hit him with the broom. He's probably got a sliver
from the broom stuck in his mouth.'

'When did Jennifer hit him with the broom?'

'Just before we left. She was playing with him, trying to scare
him with the broom. She hit him by accident and he yelped. Look
at him! He's definitely not himself.'

'We'll be in Canada tomorrow. Let's wait till then. We'll take
him to a vet in the Sault.'

59
Grape Pudding

A man in a track suit had been running along the pathways of the
park all afternoon. Running methodically around and around as
if he were in training for a marathon run. He wore a T-shirt with
ATWOOD ATHLETIC CLUB printed on it. He seemed serious,
mechanical, inhuman. I read his mind. It was a total vacuum.

While making sandwiches and tea I quietly observed a family
of campers nearby. At first I thought it was an acquaintance of

mine, Tom Ruffo, and his family. The guy was the same shape and size as Tom, a little too neatly dressed and groomed. I was just about to holler over Hey Tom, when I remembered it couldn't be Tom and it certainly wasn't his family because his family was dead and Tom was in jail in Hamilton awaiting trial on a charge of murdering them. The papers were full of this gory murder, with bodies popping up all over Southern Ontario.

Anyway, as I prepared lunch, the guy kept yelling at his daughter. His wife just sat there patiently while the guy seemed on the verge of losing his mind.

'*Michelle, stop that,*' he yelled. The little girl started crying. She was only about two and a half.

A few minutes later the little girl started pushing her doll buggy. 'Michelle, come here. Come here right now!' The guy slapped her on the behind and said, 'How many times do I have to tell you to stop pushing your stroller?' Michelle burst into tears again. His wife just sat there.

I took the tea and sandwiches down to Joan and the kids who were sitting on the beach. There was a lot of stillness in the air. An hour passed without us being aware of time. We watched the gulls floating in the golden air. We watched the sailboats, the occasional swimmer. We watched the changing sky, the bleeding sun, the softening light.

A steamer must have been passing through the straits but it was too far out to see. The smoke rose from an invisible point and became a lovely banner of pink in the setting sun. The sun was all red and gold and the clouds were like grape pudding. And somewhere someone must have flicked a switch because suddenly the massive bridge vanishing in the misty distance became illuminated and the shape of the bridge became delineated by a thousand stationary lights as well as by the moving lights of the tiny cars and trucks passing over it.

I was so proud of my fire-building abilities. 'Building a fire is like writing,' I thought out loud.

'You can say that again,' said Joan, startling me, the flames mysteriously flickering in her eyes.

'There are no two fires alike and never have been. If you think two fires are alike look more closely.'

'That's right. Everything's different. Just like writing,' said Joan. She was being sarcastic but I didn't care.

'Timing of course is everything,' I said. 'You have to get the right piece of wood ignited at precisely the right moment, the match on

60
What Writing Is Like

the paper, the twigs, the pieces of dried bark, the larger twigs, the softwood logs and finally the hardwood logs. And the better you make it the longer it'll last.'

'Just like writing,' said Joan, yawning. She once sent one of her poems to the novelist Audrey Thomas. Audrey sent an encouraging note back but it wasn't encouraging enough for Joan. So she stopped writing.

'You can say that again.'

'And Daddy,' said Jennifer. 'There's another way it's like writing. You write on paper, right?'

'Yes?'

'And you use paper to start a fire.'

'*Right!*'

61
Mickey Mouse

Joan and the kids climbed into the van to sleep. It was dark. I sat by the fire reading Rabelais. Everything went still and it appeared as if everyone in the state park, if not in the entire state, was asleep. After a while I noticed a skunk was lying on the ground by my feet. He must have been attracted by the fire. I felt as if I had found the perfect friend. I read for hours. I read much later than I really wanted to because I was afraid of disturbing my friend as he lay there warming himself.

Every once in a while a state trooper drove by in his cruiser.

In the morning I noticed Alison had taken a picture of Barry Manilow, the pop singer, to bed with her. It seemed like only yesterday she wouldn't go to bed without her Mickey Mouse picture. While Joan fried eggs for breakfast I played with the car radio and found a Top 40 station, WIGG from St. Ignace. Barry Manilow was singing his latest hit, inflaming teenage hearts all over the Upper Peninsula. Alison pretended she wasn't interested.

62
The Narrator Almost Becomes a Hero

I told Alison what a good singer I thought Barry Manilow was. She thought I was just teasing her at first but then when Joan joined in and said he was in the same league as such great white singers as Tony Bennett and Peggy Lee, Alison seemed quite pleased. It was a touchy moment. Popular wisdom has it that if the parents admire a pop singer that's enough to have the child write him off. Beware of popular wisdom.

That's all that was happening when a horrendous noise broke out from the next campsite. The guy I thought was Tom Ruffo was having a vicious fight with his wife. I mean they were really fighting and shouting obscenities. I tried to ignore it but Joan started screaming, 'Oh Dave, look! He's killing her.'

I looked. The shy patient woman of yesterday was now lying on the grass and this guy kept dropping on her with his knees, bouncing up and down on her with all his weight, his knees striking her in the breasts, stomach, groin, and thighs.

What could I do? I'm a small person but with an almost perfect body, tough as a loan shark when I need to be. I ran over and grabbed him around the neck and tried to pull him off the poor woman.

The guy started swearing at me and pushing me out of the way. Then he turned and jumped on his wife again.

This time I jumped on him with all my weight and tried to pin him to the ground. He picked me up as if I were a kid but I got my right arm free and wound up and hit him in the face. Somehow, though, the punch lost momentum before connecting.

Then the guy took a similar punch at me and the same thing happened. Just before the punch landed it lost its momentum and it hardly stung at all.

'Get this turkey out of here,' the guy started screaming at no one in particular, although a small crowd had formed including some guys a lot bigger than I. His wife just lay there, patiently waiting for him to continue beating her.

Then we started squaring off and took turns punching each other in the face. Each punch landed softly somehow. No way could I really hit him. This could go on all day with neither of us getting hurt. I couldn't understand what was happening. It certainly wasn't like in the movies. Or was it?

Finally we stopped punching and just stood there staring at each other. The woman was still lying on the grass but she'd propped herself up on one elbow and was looking at us curiously. I looked at her and she gave me a dirty look as if I were the bad guy. I looked back at the guy. His face was full of hate.

'Why don't you mind your own business, you turkey?'

'You're lucky I came over. I stopped you from killing her.'

'I wasn't going to kill her. I love this woman. She's my wife. I've got a perfect right to hit her.'

Someone from the crowd put his arm around my shoulders. 'Come on, let's go. You can't win in something like this.'

I didn't know what to think. I looked down at the woman again. 'Do you want me to go?'

'Yeah, get lost you fucking asshole.'

Back at the van, Joan wanted to know if I was hurt. I said no. She gave me some fried eggs and toast. I looked back across the **71** road. The guy and his wife were holding hands and looking smug. I felt stupid.

We cleaned up the breakfast dishes and were starting to get our stuff together. We wanted to clear out in a hurry. And suddenly the wife-beater was standing there, a friendly smile on his face.

63

Pretty Soon the U.S.A. Will Be as Bad as Canada

'You're from Canada?' said the wife-beater.

I decided to return his friendliness. 'Yeah. Ever been there?'

'Hell yes. I go up there all the time on business. My boss is a Canadian himself.'

Meanwhile Bruce was at the foot of a cedar tree looking up into the branches and barking at some chipmunks. The guy went over and started tickling him behind the ears.

'Watch it. He might bite you. He's been acting kind of mean lately. I don't think he's crazy about travelling.'

'Aw, he wouldn't bite me.' The guy kept patting him. 'Would you, Bruce?' Bruce started wagging his tail in ecstasy.

So we got talking. The guy said he was from Niles, Michigan.

'That's a suburb of Chicago isn't it?'

The guy seemed insulted. 'Hell no. Chicago's on the other side of Lake Michigan. Niles is just north of South Bend, Indiana.'

So then the guy started telling me all about Canada. He was basing his remarks on a trip he took with his boss to the Maritimes.

'We kept seeing new homes being built everywhere we looked. But there didn't seem to be any people to fill the homes. There were homes for sale all over the place, but new homes kept going up. Real weird, I tell ya. So I asked my boss about it. He said no one can afford to buy homes but the government gives the builders money to build homes anyway just to keep people working. Isn't that terrible? And we're the ones who are paying for all that.'

'You said it. It's pretty bad all right.'

'And that Toronto. What a dump that is!' He looked at me. 'You're not from Toronto are you?'

'Hell no.'

'You'd have to be a pig to live there. I couldn't believe it. Garbage all over the streets. I couldn't wait to get back to the States.'

I figured it was doing the guy good to get it off his chest. And so I gave him some additional fuel by mentioning President Carter's new welfare proposals which had been announced the day before in a big speech.

'There was a big build-up for this speech on the radio,' I said.

'And then the speech started. And after about two lines they cut in with a commercial about stereo equipment. A local station cut-in. So we turned it off.'

'Yeah, well you didn't miss much. All this welfare stuff is killing us. We're the ones who are paying for it all, you and me, the workers.'

His eyes focussed a little more clearly as if he wanted to make sure I was the 'worker' type. I could read his mind. He was saying hey, maybe this guy's on welfare. He doesn't look that prosperous and his van's a wreck. He doesn't have Bermuda shorts and a golf cap. But I smiled back encouragingly, his eyes went blurry again and he continued his tirade.

'Pretty soon it'll be as bad down here as what you've got up there in Canada. What's that guy's name – Trudeau? – that son-of-a-bitch Commie.'

The trees shimmered in the summer breeze. The guy started patting Bruce again. It was weird standing there talking to the guy without referring to the fight we'd had, or to what I thought was practically the attempted murder of his wife. I wasn't going to say anything – but suddenly I was just blurting it out.

'You're going to kill your wife one of these days you know. Grow up and stop taking all your silly frustrations out on her. She's not responsible for the new welfare proposals or for the garbage in the streets of Toronto.'

The guy's expression didn't change. He had a little smile on his face.

'I'd never kill my wife. I love her.'

'It looked to me like you were trying to kill her.'

'Never. We both push each other around at times. But we love each other.'

'*You* were doing all the pushing around. She wasn't fighting back at all. And what about little Michelle? She doesn't very often push you back. How old is she? Two? Three?'

'You keep Michelle out of it, you hear?'

Just then Michelle walked up and started looking at the cross around my neck, the one that Jennifer found on the path while searching for mushrooms.

'Daddy, why is he wearing that cross?'

Daddy looked a little embarrassed. I looked down as if I'd just noticed it hanging there.

'It's to ward off mushroom poisoning,' I said. 'It's a good luck charm. I'm superstitious. Do you know what superstitious means?'

'No.'

'It means I believe in magic.'

We drove into St. Ignace then got on the Interstate 75 heading north to the Sault. What a boring, business-like highway! We got sick of it after a mile or two so we headed east on the U.S. 134 which follows the heavily-indented Lake Huron shore out to within a couple of nautical miles of the international border cutting through Potoganissing Bay. In fact from De Tour Village, on the eastern tip of Michigan's Upper Peninsula, you can see St. Joseph Island which is in Canada.

From De Tour Village you can get a ferry to Drummond Island, a fairly large island on the U.S. side. Across from Drummond Island is Cockburn Island which is on the Canadian side. Next to that is Manitoulin Island.

We passed a sign advertising a marathon race that was being held that afternoon on Drummond Island. Joan thought it might be worth crossing on the ferry to see the race. 'Maybe that's what that guy was practising for last night,' she said.

We were driving past a lot of coves with beautiful sandy beaches a hundred feet wide. The water looked warm and shallow but there was no one around. No footprints in the sand except for those left by families of Canada geese who seemed to be standing around in a trance. There were occasional fishermen sitting in boats among the reeds with long bamboo poles. And there were lots of islands, rock outcroppings with some stunted cedars twisted by the wind. It looked like driving along the north shore of the St. Lawrence River east of Gananoque and seeing the beginning of the Thousand Islands.

We passed a large grey barn with a sign saying WEEKLY WAVE. 'Wonder what that is?'

'That's a hairdressing establishment.'

'Oh, I thought it was the local newspaper.'

We passed a sign saying CEDAR CAMPUS — IVP WRITERS WELCOME. There was a narrow road leading off into the woods.

'Hey, I'm a writer. Should we investigate?'

'No.'

We stopped at a roadside park dedicated to Hubert H. Humphrey.

'It's so beautiful around here but so desolate. I wonder why everyone doesn't come here.'

'I don't know.'

The park was full of huge chunks of granite. There were oak trees, birch, and clumps of spruce and pine. We ran down to the beach. There was a rowboat sitting there complete with oars. We decided against taking it out for a ride. Wordsworth would have.

There were some clumps of long white flower-like fungi. I remembered seeing them when I was a kid but I had no idea what they were called. I had an idea they were edible. They grew something like fiddleheads but were pure white, with sort of a greasy consistency, a mushroom-like flesh. As they grew they pushed aside thick heavy layers of dead wet leaves, just pushed them aside like flaps in a carpet. They had a semi-foetid smell. They weren't in any of our mushroom books. I decided to pick a few specimens and try to get them identified.

In the washroom someone had written SHOW HARD ON FOR A BLOW JOB. Under that, in another hand, some more literate person had written TO WHOM? And, in a third hand, TO THE YARDMAN ON WEDNESDAY.

There was a cute eighteen-year-old attendant in the gas station in De Tour Village. 'You put it in there,' I said, pointing to my gas tank.

'I know, I know,' she said. 'Women can pump gas just as well as men.' Her breasts were bouncing attractively.

When she finished some gas spilled down the side of the car. 'See this?' I said. I pointed to it.

'Yeah?'

'You think I'm gonna pay for that?'

The gauge was just a fraction over $8.72. 'I'll tell you what,' she said. 'I'll only charge you $8.72.'

'Oh. That's okay then.' She laughed in an exaggerated fashion and grabbed my arm. 'Don't touch me,' I said. 'My wife'll kill you. She's so jealous.'

'Aw, it must be awful for you.'

I went in the little office to pay her. On the wall was a photo of an old guy in traditional service station uniform. Under the picture were the words IN MEMORIAM RUSSELL L. SCHOPP. AWARDED FOR FIFTY YEARS OF SERVICE TO THE MOTORING PUBLIC. The guy bore a certain family resemblance to the girl.

'Is that your grandfather?'

'Yes.'

'You look like him.'

'Really? Do I?'

'Yup.' She looked pleased. 'How long's he been dead?'

'About five years.'

'Do you think you'll ever get an award for fifty years of service to the motoring public?'

65
Fifty Years of Service to the Motoring Public

'No way, Jose.'

Then I noticed her father. He was in the garage working on a car. He'd stopped work and was glaring at me. I guess he figured I was getting too friendly with his daughter. So before leaving I asked her about Drummond Island.

'I don't know', she said. 'It's pretty much the same over there as it is here'. She said she'd never heard of any marathon race.

66
On the Road to the Sault

Quite a few cars were lined up like sheep at the ferry terminal. We decided not to visit Drummond Island. We were getting a little tired of the American side. We drove out of town and headed along a series of country roads cross-country towards Sault Ste. Marie.

We passed through Goetzville, Raber, Stalwart, Stirlingville, Pickford. We saw an old log cabin being pulled down the road by a truck. We started singing. *The old log cabin, it just keeps rolling along.*

Dotted with farms and villages the countryside was flat but warped slightly like a piece of plywood so that without realizing you'd been climbing you found yourself at times able to see incredible distances from a gentle height. At one point we could see three villages, the shadows of small clouds crossing the land like ugly omens of the future.

The area was fairly prosperous but untouched by the modern era. Sections were heavily wooded. It could have been 1930. It was a little like Manitoulin Island but there were no abandoned farms visible. At one point Joan asked me to stop. There were some interesting weeds at the roadside.

'You don't see these kinds of weeds in Canada.'

'Sure you do.'

'No you don't.'

'I see weeds like that all over the place in Canada.'

'No you don't.'

'Sure I do. Bigger specimens too.'

Joan was getting angry. She got out of the car and picked an armful. She had about nine different varieties, none of which she could identify. She wanted to dry them out, identify them and use them in her flower-arranging class.

She was just getting back in the car with her armful of weeds when the car inexplicably rolled back a few inches. Honest, I didn't do it on purpose. Joan started screaming.

'Dave! Stop! You're driving over my foot!'

I slammed on the brakes.

'Daddy, you rolled over Mommy's foot.'

'Oh, oh! Is she all right?'

Joan got in the car.

'Are you all right?'

'Jesus Christ, you're stupid today. You rolled right over my foot. You're lucky I'm wearing these clogs.'

'I'm lucky? You're lucky you mean.'

'Daddy! Jeez, the least you could do is say you're sorry.'

'Oh yeah. I'm sorry, Joan. I don't know how that happened. Are there any bones broken?'

'I don't think so but it's awfully sore.' She put her foot up on my knee. I looked at it. Sure enough there was a black tire mark, a series of wiggly parallel black lines, over the arch of her foot. I massaged it and she didn't cry out so I figured she was okay. We drove off.

Just then a turkey vulture, the colour of a tire mark, flew low over the car. It kept crossing and recrossing the road at a height of about thirty feet. We were driving about twenty miles an hour and it was keeping just ahead of us, zigzagging back and forth across the road, its wings held motionless in a broad v.

'Oh Dave, it's beautiful.'

It was joined by another. They kept in front of us, flying in tandem, for several miles. Abruptly they flew off into the woods.

We started driving faster and a few miles later another turkey vulture appeared just in front of us and flew along with us for a mile or so before disappearing. Joan was getting quite excited.

We had crossed a height of land and suddenly we could see for miles ahead. There were a pair of turkey vultures on the road ahead of us and so I braked, cut the motor and coasted slowly and silently towards them. They were eating a dead animal. There was no other traffic.

It seemed wrong that they should be called turkey vultures. It's certainly not the name they would give themselves supposing they felt a need to give themselves a name. They were certainly more interesting and much more beautiful than turkeys, and they flew a lot better than any turkey I'd ever seen. They're closer to a condor although more plentiful. But because of the red wattles around the head they were stuck with this derogatory name. The Latin name, *Cathartes aura,* is much nicer.

As we coasted closer we could see they were more brown than black in colour. We were scarcely breathing, just as in flight their wings scarcely fluttered. The kids had climbed up front to get a good view of them. We were just inching ahead. And then without turning their heads to look at us they took to the air.

At that moment there was a loud rustling noise to our right. We **77** looked, and a great blue heron with a six-foot wingspan was rising from a marshy area at the side of the road. It was less than thirty feet away. Joan was in ecstasy.

'Oh Dave, how incredible! Look at the way it flies.'

It lifted off like a basketball player and the sound it made was like the sound of a cheering crowd.

67
How to Become Strong

Another of those coincidences that leave you a little unsteady. No sooner had I typed out the above title than I flicked on the radio, something I seldom do when I'm working. And someone was talking about Jamaican reggae music and Rastafarian culture in general. How the dreadlocks are intended to give the appearance of a lion and to confuse your enemies into not knowing whether you're coming or going.

'When you get down and you quarrel every day, you're prayin' to the devils I say.' That's from 'Rastafarian Vibrations,' a Bob Marley song from the time before Marley became commercial under pressure from the nervous American record distributors who were concerned about his Jamaican nationalism which of course has certain anti-American strains as has any nationalism in the twentieth century except of course American nationalism. How to become strong.

The guy on the radio was saying that he was at a Bob Marley concert in Kingston and Marley spotted the prime minister and the leader of the opposition in different parts of the audience. He also spotted the rival leaders of two of Kingston's deadliest gangs. So he called all four to the stage and made them all join hands and sing 'One Love.' How to become strong.

Back to the story. We could feel the electromagnetic presence of Sault Ste. Marie over the horizon, sending out signals, lines of force. 'I've got a riddle, everyone,' I said. 'What do Niagara Falls, Ontario, and Sault Ste. Marie, Ontario, have in common?'

'That's easy,' said Joan. 'They're both border cities and there are cities of the same name on the other side.'

'If Canada and the Unites States joined up do you think the two Niagara Falls would become one and the two Sault Ste. Maries?'

'No.'

'Why not?'

'The local politicians would convince everyone it wouldn't be in the best civic interests when all they really were worried about would be losing their jobs and influence.'

'You've got a point there.' How to become strong.

78   I began thinking that when a Canadian visits Sault Ste. Marie,

Michigan, or Niagara Falls, New York, it's as if he's visiting another universe, a universe of anti-matter. One almost expects every building, every inhabitant of the city on the Canadian side to have its easily identifiable counterpart on the American side. Instead he feels as if he's descended into some kind of hell, a hell that is all the more hellish because it resembles so strongly on the surface the world he has known. In fact it has the same name. The power of a name.

And there is a darkness here. Niagara Falls, New York, and Sault Ste. Marie, Michigan, are always darker and colder than their Canadian twins. Even when you approach from the American side as we were approaching Sault Ste. Marie, Michigan, after travelling slowly up the American side of Lake Huron, there is a feeling that Sault Ste. Marie, Ontario, once it's reached, will be surrounded with an unearthly light, or at least an earthly light that has been blocked by the figure of the self in an alien ground.

For an American visiting Sault Ste. Marie, Ontario, or Niagara Falls, Ontario, it might be that the opposite would hold. For them, Canada seems a poverty-stricken carnival mirror image of the United States. Even the poets, the ones you most want to trust, betray their national origin when they speak of Canada. It's as if the United States were wearing a rented hat. Or perhaps a borrowed hat.

Walt Whitman said it was inevitable that Canada be liberated. Even the enlightened Charles Olson said Canada should be annexed immediately (I've never seen the quote but that's what people tell me). William Carlos Williams would have been embarrassed to think that any *Canadian* was reading him with serious intent. And of course towards the end when he realized he'd become a famous poet his stuff did become more international in flavour. The way you talk in your own house and the way you talk outside. As for Robert Duncan he said no one could ever accuse him of cultural imperialism because he'd been telling Canadian audiences for years to write about their own roots. Of course roots are something different to a poet and to his audience. They don't necessarily mean ancestry and environment. How the self is rooted to the flesh. How the flesh is rooted in the flesh of others. How the individual mind is rooted in the communal mind. How the communal mind is rooted in other communal minds. How other communal minds are rooted in nature. How nature is rooted in existence. How time is rooted in space. How space is rooted in poetry. How Bob Marley got those people up on the stage to sing 'One Love'. How to become strong.

Yet the best poets of the strong countries of the world must always be read and taken seriously by the best poets of the weaker countries of the world for deeply buried in the writing of the best poets of the strong countries lies the key to survival for the poets of the weaker countries. We're talking about the real poets, not the popular puppets who seem to be personifications of all that is glorious in the national psyche. Rather it's the seers, the Garcia Lorcas, Frank O'Haras, Jack Spicers, the ones who are often rejected by that which tends to repress weakness in a strong country. Among the things that such a country represses is the machinery, the paraphernalia of their own essential weakness. That weakness must be seized and understood. Only in that way will we become strong. Perhaps I shouldn't say 'only'.

I almost didn't use this piece because although I remember knowing what I was talking about when I wrote it in my notebook during the trip I'm not sure I know now what it was I was talking about. But that's just my own weakness. If it was true once it will always be true – to someone. As if I knew how to become strong.

Being up front with weakness is a strengthening process. And not being concerned with strength or weakness. Not being concerned with yourself as something separate or separatable from what surrounds you.

68
The Department of Natural Resources

We rejoined the famous Interstate 75 just south of Sault Ste. Marie and we could feel Canada up there, a goal to reach, a symbol of freedom and wide open spaces, the end of the Underground Railroad. It was as if we were ants walking along a wall and suddenly confronting the frame of a painting.

Heading into the Sault we passed a nice-looking building on a hill. There were flowers and trees in the lawn out front. A sign indicated it was the field headquarters for the Michigan Department of Natural Resources.

'Here's our chance to get our specimens identified', I said. On the other side of the road and down a bit was a gift shop built to resemble a log cabin.

'Why don't you drop us off at that shop', said Joan, 'then go back and get the stuff identified and then pick us up?'

'But what about your weeds? Wouldn't you rather have them identified than go shopping in a dumb little store like that?'

'You can get them identified for me.'

'We'll be in Canada in an hour and you can spend your money there.'

'I just want to see what's in the store.'
'Okay.'
'But don't be too long.'
'Why not?'
'I'm anxious to get into Canada.'
'Why?'
'We have to get Bruce to the vet's. Remember?'

There were quite a few cars in the parking lot, but there didn't seem to be that many people inside the building itself. Maybe they were all hiding until five o'clock. Maybe they were playing pinochle in the basement.

There was a young couple poring over some topographical maps of the region. They were being assisted by a uniformed staff member. It seems the couple had bought a tract of land sight unseen and were now having trouble locating it.

I plunked the weeds and fungus specimens on the counter. The fungus was beginning to turn black. The staff member was a tall brown-haired guy about twenty-four years old.

The couple put down their map. They were suddenly more interested in the plant material. I held up one of the fungi. 'I wonder if it would be possible to get this identified.'

The guy in the uniform took the plant from my hand. 'Hm,' he said. His eyes were blank. It was obvious he didn't get requests of this nature often. In the United States most people don't expect the government to know anything.

'I think it's pretty common,' I said. 'It just bugs me that I don't know what it is. Any ideas?'

'Well, I've seen it before but I don't know.'

'Do you have any books on fungi or mushrooms?'

The guy reached under the counter and pulled out a leaflet. Wouldn't you know it was the same one I'd seen in Michigan state parks all along the Lake Huron shore. It was called *Michigan's Morels and Wildflowers* and was put out by the Michigan Tourist Council and Department of Natural Resources. On one side there were pictures of ten different kinds of morels and an article on morels by William J. Mullendore. On the other side were pictures and descriptions of eleven different wildflowers and an article by R.D. Burroughs. There was a little ad in one corner stating that 'this folder is a reprint from *Michigan Natural Resources,* the colorful, authentic, non-profit, no-advertising, bimonthly magazine of the state Department of Natural Resources. For a year's **81** subscription send $3 to Michigan Natural Resources, Lansing, Michigan, 48926. It's the last big magazine bargain in North America.'

'No', he said. 'I'm afraid this is all we've got.'

'And I guess there's no way we could get these weeds identified?'

'Afraid not. Sorry.'

The couple with the map were just standing there.

'We've got some books in the car that might be of some help', said the woman. 'You know where they are don't you, Roger?'

'Good idea', said Roger. 'Be back in a minute.'

When Roger returned he had a pile of books on mushrooms, fungi and wildflowers. The fungus was easy to identify. It was the *Monotrepa uniflora,* commonly known as Indian Pipe. A member of the Wintergreen family, it grows everywhere from June to September. Everywhere in North America that is. The fact that the Indian Pipe was turning black was a positive guide to identification. Like many fungi they turn black when touched. Some psilocybin mushrooms turn blue or purple.

We could only identify one of the weeds. It was the Meadow Parsnip. There was a picture of it in the *Field Guide to Waterflowers.*

'Well, thanks for all your help', I said.

'Don't mention it.'

70
The Body of Someone You Love

Sault Ste. Marie, Michigan, has its own little CN Tower. It's made of wood. It's actually an observation tower about a hundred feet high from which you can see presumably the Sault locks and a wide expanse of Canada across the St. Mary River. But it was closed down. Funny that it would be closed in the tourist season. There was a fence around it, the door was heavily padlocked and there was barbed wire strung all the way around. It looked like an ammo dump in Vietnam. The wooden stairs leading up to the tower, winding around and around, looked rotten. Maybe somebody had taken a fall and that's why the thing was closed to the public.

All along the riverfront was a US Navy installation. We drove through the town. Joan showed what she bought in the store that looked like a log cabin. It was a plaque with three mushrooms painted on it. The mushrooms had orange caps, yellow gills and yellow stems.

'That'll look really nice in the kitchen.'

'But I bought it for your room.'

From the International Bridge we looked down and saw the rapids far below. 'Now we're in Canada,' I said.

'It looks just like the United States,' said Alison.

'It does?'

'Yeah. It's the same kind of concrete on the bridge.'

'Can't you feel a difference in the air?'

'Yeah, I guess you can. A little.'

There was a long line-up of cars at customs. I'd flown into Sault Ste. Marie a couple of times but just on brief stopovers. Yet already I felt as if we'd come home. It wasn't that we were back in familiar territory. But it was as if we'd arrived back in the kind of strangeness we were accustomed to. No one could ever live long enough to become really familiar with a country the size of Canada. Canada will always be strange. But at least it's my strangeness, the strangeness I'm familiar with. The kind of strangeness that is like the body of someone you love, the kind of strangeness you feel free to explore as intimately as you want without feeling awkward or self-conscious about it.

The rapids of the St. Mary River are a mile wide. We drove around under the International Bridge to have a look at the dock and lock area and at an old power dam that looked as if it had been old when Charles Sangster was a fledgling. I know this is totally ridiculous but I just felt like getting out of the car and rubbing up against the walls and telephone poles and phone booths. It was so nice to be back in Canada. The last refuge of the scoundrel and all that. How embarrassing! But you have to be truthful about these things.

71
How to Become Strange

We went further out along a dead end river road under the International Bridge and stopped so Joan could get out and have a pee behind some bushes. Just as she was having her pee a big excursion boat came around the corner. It was loaded with passengers. They started pointing at Joan and laughing. Passengers came running around from the other side of the boat, which began threatening to capsize.

Joan was infuriated. She wiggled her pink bum back into her jeans and stumbled into the van, her face crimson. 'Jesus Christ,' she said. 'Canada is supposed to be the most sparsely populated country in the world and you can't even find a place to pee in private.'

As we sped away we could still see the people on the boat laughing their fool heads off.

Bruce was sitting on the table looking quite blasé as the vet looked at his ears.

'They're inflamed all right.'

This was Dr. S.M. Yogi. His office was on the side of the Trans-Canada Highway a few miles north of Sault Ste. Marie, Ontario.

Dr. Yogi was an Asian Indian as was Dr. Swami. Dr. Swami you will recall was the guy who stitched Jennifer's wounds after Bruce bit her. That was in Tawas City, Michigan, a couple of hundred miles south of the Sault. Yet by one of those strange coincidences that plague my life, Dr. Yogi not only resembled Dr. Swami but he even had a similar heart-shaped birthmark between his eyes.

'Would the inflammation be severe enough to cause him to bite a child?'

'He'll certainly be in a better temper once the inflammation is cleared up.'

He gave us a bottle of eardrop fluid. Then he gave Bruce his annual rabies shot. Then he went into a long discourse on animal psychology.

'To Bruce, Jennifer is the runt of the litter. With many dogs they have to have someone to pick on and it's often the runt of the litter that gets it the worst. To Bruce, the members of the family are his litter and Jennifer, being the smallest member of the family, is the runt.'

He went on and on in this vein. He finally came up with a good suggestion. He suggested that Jennifer be the one to feed Bruce. And that she take Bruce for walks more frequently. Since she is the runt it was necessary for her to take greater pains to be friends with Bruce.

'Do you hear that, Jennifer?'

'Yes.' Her eyes were smouldering with seriousness. 'Can I take him for a walk right now?'

The vet charged us twenty bucks. In the waiting room was a wide assortment of dogs and cats and people. Joan was talking to a woman with a black Norwegian elkhound named Smokey. It thought it was pregnant.

'It's false pregnancy. She gets like this once a year at least.'

The dog looked so mournful. The woman had provided a little stuffed pup for it to play with. The dog was lying on the floor with the pup between its forelegs, gently cradling it.

The woman said she was from Hamilton too. She'd been living for the past two months in a logging camp cabin with her husband somewhere in the back woods. But their cabin had burnt to the ground earlier that week while they were in town at a bingo game. She was German, six feet tall, strong-looking. She looked as if she'd been working hard, her face tanned and leathery, her large man-like hands gnarled and fingernails black. Yet she was totally feminine, exuding a strong female radiance.

'I'm heading back to Hamilton as soon as I get her looked after,' she said, nodding at the dog. 'I'm sick of the north woods. I want to open a corner jug milk store.'

73
The Raw Material of My Life

We were on the Trans-Canada Highway heading south around Lake George. We passed over the Garden River which flows down through the Garden River Indian Reserve into the north channel of the St. Mary River. On the abutment of a train bridge someone had painted THIS IS INDIAN TERRITORY and INDIAN POWER.

We still hadn't decided whether to travel all the way around Georgian Bay or cut down through Manitoulin Island then take the ferry to Tobermory on the Bruce Peninsula.

The kids wanted to take the ferry. As I drove along I tried to invoke a precognitive vision of this book. If I could see it clearly enough I could flip the pages and find out which route we should take by simply reading in the book which route we'd taken. I'd been writing for a long time out of the raw material of my life. It was beginning to seem as if my life was following my writing rather than the other way around. It was as if the writing came first and the circumstances of my life were merely mechanisms to bring the writing into existence from the place in eternity where it had always existed. I wouldn't say anything about that to Joan. She'd give me hell for being too pretentious. But you understand, don't you?

74
The New Bridge to St. Joseph Island

We decided to spend some time on St. Joseph Island. The bridge had only been open a year or so. Before that the residents had to rely on a ferry in the summer and skating across in the winter. When the bridge was open the way of life changed quickly. People who lived and worked on the mainland built permanent homes on the island. It was quite a shock to some of the old-timers who'd been living in isolation all their lives. Some were third generation islanders.

It was like the shock that befell the fishermen of the upper Great Lakes when the Welland Canal first opened. Niagara Falls had proven a formidable barrier for the sea lamprey. Suddenly they were free to surge into Lakes Erie, Huron, Michigan and Superior, and the huge lake trout fishing industry was destroyed almost overnight.

It was a neat bridge. The road forms a causeway of sorts connecting several small, rocky, spruce-clad islands in the stream before taking to the air and crossing the main channel on seven concrete supports.

The island is encircled by a road. It's called Highway 548. When we got off the bridge we didn't waste any time figuring out whether to travel clockwise or counterclockwise around the island. Whether we went left or right would have a strong influence on this part of the book. So we simply turned left and decided to go clockwise.

The first town we came to was Hilton Beach. It was like being in Burlington, Ontario, in 1900.

75
Burlington, Ontario

In the dry goods store at the main intersection of Hilton Beach several elderly women in frilly dresses crowded around us when we said we were looking for a nice place to eat. They seemed to come from the back of the store, the attic, the basement. It was strange.

But we didn't need to feel threatened. They merely recommended the Hilton Beach Hotel at the waterfront.

There was a clean tablecloth and a bowl of fresh flowers at our ordinary kitchen table in the dining room of the hotel. Through the window we could see a small dock and the low forested hills of Northern Ontario dimly across the wide immensity of the swiftly flowing St. Joseph Channel. It must have been a long way to skate for provisions.

We looked at the menu and ordered the baked ham dinner, all except Jennifer who wanted a hamburger. The waitress was about seventeen. When she retreated into the kitchen I said something to the effect that the girl probably goes to high school and works here part time.

'I'm not going to work part-time when I go to high school,' said Jennifer. 'It's no fun.'

I got thinking about Burlington, Ontario. If in 1900, seventy-seven years ago, Burlington, Ontario, looked like Hilton Beach does now, which it did, then in seventy-seven years from now, by the year 2054, Hilton Beach will look like Burlington, Ontario, does now.

If you've never seen Burlington, Ontario, it's just another one of those huge suburban cities that exploded out of a nice small town over the past thirty years. Everyone works in Toronto or Hamilton, commuting by Go Train or car in a twice-a-day ritual of mind-destroying boredom. It makes Delta, B.C., seem like paradise.

In the case of Burlington you can still see what the original town must have been like if you wander down to the waterfront. You can see the nice old houses and commercial blocks at what was then the main corner of town. But now you can drive for an hour in any direction from that point and still be in Burlington, a Mississauga-like maze of style-less houses, gas stations, junk food outlets, muffler shops and shopping centres. It's sort of a cultural collision between the Mafia and Simpsons-Sears.

But a lot of people like Burlington. People who live there by and large love it. The poet George Bowering once said that if he had to live in just one place for the rest of his life he would want that place to be Burlington, Ontario. A great tribute to a great little city.

I guess it's about time I broke into the present again. I was hoping to be able to get through the whole book without once breaking into the present but as you know if you're reading consecutively – and I sincerely hope you are – I didn't make it. And once you start you must keep it up.

When I'm writing verse I break into the present a lot but not when I'm writing prose. Joan's Uncle Albert died last night, of cancer, at 53. He was a man whom children loved. He was a particular favourite of Jennifer. In the last half-hour of his life his pain suddenly stopped, his breathing relaxed, his twitchings stopped and a tremendous peace fell upon him. According to those who were there he remained conscious until the point of death.

He worked at the glass works in Hamilton and was a union official. His big project was establishing a social centre for retired union members. He put an incredible amount of time into it and when people asked him why he said it was for selfish reasons, he wanted to be able to have a social centre to come to when he retired. Dead at 53.

His fellow workers raised $6,000 to send Albert to the Bahamas for a cancer treatment. When he returned he was convinced he was cured. Even when the cancer started breaking out again he thought it was something else.

Why does this breaking into the writer's present circumstances occur less frequently in prose than in verse? Because in prose one's attention is fascinated by a story line while in verse one's

76
A Damsel in Eternal Distress

attention is taken up with the music. Even if the verse takes a narrative form the story is secondary. Verse is simply more interesting than prose. Trying to remain submerged in the writing without reference to the present when you're writing poetry is like trying to sleep when your room is filled with beautiful, interesting people.

Of course I'm open to misinterpretation here. As a reader you might argue that prose is more interesting than verse. It certainly sells better. Fiction outsells poetry twenty to one according to David Kerfoot of Duthie Books in Vancouver. However that's because fiction usually attracts the more interesting writers, the livelier minds. Poetry has become like macramé. A craft that anyone can do, a craft aimed at an audience of two. A lot of small Canadian publishers are refusing to publish poetry. As they say at Coach House Press, one prose writer is worth a gross of poets. But just because the general run of poets are betraying poetry doesn't mean that poetry is something less interesting than prose. It's just waiting for someone to rescue it again, a damsel in eternal distress.

77
The Plot to Strip Us of Our Beauty

Imagine a man sitting at a table with a beautiful woman and two beautiful pubescent girls. And he falls in love with the waitress.

She said she was sad that the ferry was gone. She said it was now in use in Kingston, Ontario taking cars and people over to Wolfe Island. She said her big ambition was to travel to Kingston and take one last trip on it.

I shuddered with sympathy. I had to fight the urge to take her to one side and say, 'Look. I'm going to drive my wife and kids to the nearest bus terminal and send them home. And I'll be right back to take you to Kingston.' But the forces of good once again defeated the forces of evil.

Bridges are beautiful but ferry boats are almost always more beautiful. And the replacement of ferry boats by bridges is all part of the evolutionary plot to strip us of our beauty, and thereby perhaps increase our sense of beauty, our discovery of beauty inside ourselves. This plot has been unfolding for thousands of years. Look at the Acropolis, or some other magnificent structure of antiquity. These were the products of a communal mind so utterly different from ours as to be unimaginable. A mind for whom beauty was an inevitable part of expression. A mind for whom the Homeric line was ordinary speech.

88   Eventually bridges will be replaced by tunnels. And people will be banding together to protest the tearing down of old McDonald chain restaurants.

'We used to know everyone on the island,' the girl said. She just stood there looking at me, her eyes glued to mine. She knew I understood the feelings behind her words. 'But not now.'

In the front part of the hotel was a bar room where a lot of people were sitting around drinking beer. 'Out of all the people in there how many would you know by name?'

'Probably none.'

The current of the St. Joseph Channel swept by relentlessly outside the window. Two hundred years ago it was the route of the voyageurs on their way into Indian territory to return with furs to make hats for the beautiful gentlemen of Europe. Great mythic adventures. Right across from us were the towns of Desbarats and Bruce Mines. Desbarats is where the waitress went to high school. She pronounced it Deborah.

We ate our ham, with homemade soup and blueberry pie fresh from the oven. There was a watercolour on the wall showing the same view we had from the window except that the dock in the foreground was shaped a little different. It was pointing the other way. We asked the waitress about it.

78
An Unsigned Watercolour

She said the painting was done by a woman from Toronto who used to vacation at St. Joseph Island in the 1940s and often stayed at the Hilton Beach Hotel. The waitress was too young to have known her but she knew of her.

She said the dock shown in the painting had been wrecked in a storm and a new one built recently. The new dock was pointing a different way but the hills on the north shore of the passage were just the same.

'That's a good painting. What was the woman's name?'

'I can't remember. She was pretty old then. She's probably dead now.'

We left Hilton Beach and drove over to the eastern part of the island, to the Mosquito Bay area, along a narrow, winding, hilly highway which cuts through dense woods. At one point we parked the van and walked into the woods to see what it looked like in there.

79
On the Road to Whisky Bay

The kids pretended they were frightened. I found a World War ii army helmet that had been blasted with a hunter's shotgun and was rusting out. I thought someone had been using it to collect berries in 1949 and had left it behind and someone else had been using it for target practice. The woods were mysterious, maybe because of the isolated nature of the island. I kept thinking we were about to be ambushed by a family of wild mutants or Scottish cannibals or that we were going to come upon a miraculous child wandering around in a daze.

We drove south from Mosquito Bay and across the Kaskawan River and then along Tenby Bay. Without the map we wouldn't have had a clue which direction we were going in or where we were. The road maintains a respectful distance from the shoreline, which is mostly private and taken up by American cottagers, and there are few signposts.

But when we got to the end of the road we knew if we turned left we'd end up at Whisky Bay and so we did.

80

The Cold Waters of Potoganissing Bay

And suddenly the interminable woods opened up and we were driving down a hill to the shore. There was a white frame house, a lot of trailers parked around, some outbuildings, and a dock. It was beginning to get dark and some campers were starting a campfire. All the camping trailers and vans boasted American flags and American licence plates. The campfire wasn't going very good so someone doused the flames with lighting fluid then jumped back. Someone else had a huge string of big fat fish.

We immediately felt out of place. For one thing we were Canadians. I think it's natural for a Canadian to feel more out of place in a part of Canada which has been taken over by Americans than he would say in the United States. And then we weren't interested in fishing. So it looked as if we'd come to the wrong place. But it was getting dark and we didn't want to go any further. There is no such thing as a wrong place for a writer, especially one as all-fired serious as I was.

So I went into the office-cum-store and took a campsite for the night. The woman had bad breath and wasn't very friendly. I had the feeling she'd had reports on us all along the road from Hilton Beach and knew we were coming, a family of Canadians. Possibly bad for business. In the back room children were crying and funny smells wafted out through the open door.

After we got settled Joan started reading the kids a story and I walked down to the dock. A cabin cruiser was coming in after a day's fishing. A male and female in their early twenties were aboard. They looked quite simple-minded in a violent sort of way. They overshot the dock and it looked as if their boat was going to plough into another boat and cause some damage.

I jumped off the dock into the boat they were rushing towards. I reached out and stopped their boat as it was about to collide. I don't know how I managed to avoid breaking my arm but the tactic worked. There was no collision. No thanks were offered, not even when the couple finally managed to get their boat parked.

'Catch any fish?' I said.

'Nah'.

We were standing on the dock. The cold waters of Potoganissing Bay surrounded us and stretched out to the horizon and disappeared between and behind wooded islands of various sizes.

And under the watery flatness we could hear huge schools of fish, giggling.

On the way back from the dock I walked through a corner of the woods and found some bright red mushrooms and picked a few to show the kids. When I got back I built a fire and we sat around it for warmth. This was the most northern part of our trip around Lake Huron and it was chilly.

81
A Small Party of American Ladies

I began reading aloud from Rabelais, the tame Cohen translation. I think I was reading Book I, Chapter 13, entitled 'How Grandgousier Realized Gargantua's Marvellous Intelligence by His Invention of an Arse-Wipe', when a small party of American ladies walked by. There were about six of them and they were dressed in pastel blue or pink pantsuits and wore their hair in perfect bouffants protected with space-age plastic hairspray. Their make-up was just so. They wore white high-heeled sandals. The wives of recreational fishermen.

As they walked along in front of us all six suddenly looked horrified and stared at the four-member McFadden family sitting around the roaring campfire. I guess they must have heard me read a nasty word. The kids were laughing their heads off at the story and the women must have been shocked that a father would read such garbage to his children. Let's face it there's something sort of communistic and unamerican about sitting around a campfire reading a *book* to your children in the first place. The proper thing to do is to take your television set with you on camping trips. But actually to read them a story about the invention of toilet paper, well that's downright atheistic.

82
Illuminated by the Flickering Light of a Dying Campfire

As the fire died I sat there wrapped in a blanket, shivering. The others were sleeping in warm sleeping bags inside the warm van.

From where I sat you could see out over the cold waters of Potoganissing Bay the twinkling lights of Drummond Island on which a marathon race was being run that night. I thought it would be nice if I could just lift off from my body and float over the waters to watch the race, to fly up behind the ear of my favourite and urge him on....

People on St. Joseph Island boasted that 'half of the states of the Union are represented on the taxpayers' rolls' and that the kids have to go to the mainland to school. I decided there was something about the island I didn't like. It was in the Canadian air that night – a sense of commercial smugness, a sense of commercial enthralment to the Americans. No one wanted to waste time with Canadians who weren't lugging big boats and who obviously didn't have buckets of money to spend. The natives wanted to be ordered around by the Americans with dune buggies and cabin cruisers and huge Winnebagos with television sets and air conditioners. They wanted to grovel in front of them. What would the original settlers have had to say about the way their grandchildren were conducting their lives?

My mushrooms were drying on the picnic table in the flickering light from the dying fire. I'd been unable to identify them even though I had some excellent guide books.

There were so many gift shops on the island. And so many abandoned farms. It just wasn't right ...

83
Elmer Trump and the Navy Bean Market

The heater in the van broke down overnight and in the morning it felt as if our bone marrow was at the point of freezing solid. I asked Joan to go out and light a fire but she refused so I had to get up.

While I was getting wood this guy came by in a green worksuit and matching hat. 'You gonna warm it up outside?' he said in an American accent. We got talking.

His name was Elmer Trump and he was from Saginaw, Michigan. He was a farmer. He grew navy beans. He had a dune buggie attached to his Winnebago. He'd towed it all the way up. I guess he was disappointed that there were no dunes on St. Joseph Island. In fact not enough beach to drive on. Just dense woods right down to the shoreline. I asked him about the market in navy beans.

'It was up to $54 a few years back but now it's down to $13.50,' he said. He seemed glad I asked. 'We've been undercut by all the

Canadian farmers getting into it once they saw it was a profitable thing.'

'Well,' I said. 'The last to get in is usually the first to get out.' I could see him pause.

Then he got talking about the cold. Turned out he was no stranger to Canada. He told me he was thinking of going in for a swim. 'I've been in water a lot colder than this,' he said.

'Oh? Where?' Thinking maybe the Arctic Ocean.

'Lake Erie. That is one cold lake, oh boy!'

Now, Lake Erie is the most shallow and warm of the five Great Lakes, and during the summer months it's warmer than the Gulf Stream. In fact there are palm trees on the south shore, as mentioned in my excellent book *A Trip around Lake Erie*. But I couldn't call him a liar. Maybe he'd been swimming in the winter. But no.

'I was swimming in Port Colborne one day,' he said. 'It was so hot under that blazing sun I dove right in. Brr. My body wanted to go back but my momentum carried me forward.'

I had the impression this was a story he'd told before. The wording was too exact. 'I've done a fair amount of swimming in Lake Erie over the years,' I said, 'and it's always pretty warm in the summer months. How long ago was this?'

He thought a minute. 'Oh about thirty years ago I guess,' he said. 'I haven't been up to Canada for a heck of a long time. Ever since they started cutting in on the navy bean market. And just about that time I'll be damned if the weather patterns didn't start changing. They started gettin' all the rain in the growin' season and we dried right up. I just don't feel like goin' to Canada any more.'

'But you're in Canada right now.'

'Well, yes. But this is different. This isn't the part where they grow things. This is just a place for ...'

'Americans to fish?'

'Yeah. Right.'

'I know.'

I was the centre of attraction, not because of my magnetic personality but because I was the only one with a fire going. Elmer and I stood there talking and keeping warm. Along came Merle, the guy who owned the place, pretending he wanted to talk. But you could see him inching closer and closer to the fire.

Merle was telling us about an elderly man who'd bought a brand new boat. He was a retired school teacher from the States.

84
Elmer's Dune Buggie

'He paid $9,000 and he wants me to launch it for him; said Merle. 'I don't think he's quite right upstairs.'

'That's the same with my dune buggie; said Elmer. 'People think I'm not right upstairs. I'm sixty-one years old you know. People want to know why I bought a dune buggie at my age. I just tell them I always wanted one and when I got the chance I bought one. How old's this teacher?'

'Seventy-two.'

85
A Study in Classic Jealousy

So Merle went down to launch the old guy's boat. We couldn't see the old guy anywhere. I made a terrible Freudian slip. 'I sure hope it sinks, I mean floats; I said.

Then another old guy came up to us at the early morning fire. At first I thought it was the guy who owned the boat but no. This guy's name was Caribou Jack, and he immediately started sneering at the unseen old guy.

'A boat that big is just to brag about; said Caribou Jack, as Merle let it drop into the water. It bounced back up and then settled in at its proper level. 'It's like catching a big fish. You can brag about it lots but you can't eat it.'

I couldn't figure out why you couldn't eat a big fish but I didn't say anything. I didn't want to appear stupid. These guys were Americans, even Caribou Jack, and even though they were guests in my own country I didn't want to give them the impression Canadians were stupid. I wanted to be a credit to my country. So I tried to look and sound as intelligent as I possibly could. Maybe big fish aren't as tasty as little ones. Maybe their meat is too tough and stringy. Maybe you can't eat them because then you wouldn't have anything to brag about. So you have to have them stuffed and shellacked and mounted on plaques on the rec room wall over the bar.

The old guy himself – the mysterious owner of the new boat – walked out on the dock. He spoke briefly to Merle in a business-like fashion. He went to get into the boat, drew back, and wiped his feet on the wooden dock. Then he got in.

'That's right; said Caribou Jack with a mean look on his face. 'That's right. Wipe your feet you silly old bastard. I know people who have *million*-dollar boats. That's nothing.' This was turning into a study in classic jealousy. The kind of hatred that you seldom hear expressed so eloquently. Usually it just eats away silently at people's hearts.

'Have you got a boat yourself?' I said.

'Yeah.' Something had gone out of his voice.

'Where is it?' I said softly, after ten seconds of silence.

'It's over there.'

I looked. 'Where?'

'Behind the dock.'

I couldn't see any boats behind the dock so I figured it must have been a pretty small boat. The dock only came about thirty inches out of the water. His boat must have been smaller than that.

'I don't see any boat behind the dock.'

'It's right behind the dock. You can't see it from here.'

It turned out to be a little rowboat he'd brought up on his car-top carrier all the way from his home in Royal Oak, Michigan. He kept talking out of the side of his mouth, like Henry Miller. He was a short, skinny guy in his sixties. I asked him what his name was.

'Jack,' he said. 'They call me Caribou Jack way up in Canada.'

Like Elmer Trump, Caribou Jack seemed to have forgotten we were in Canada. Then again we were only a few miles from the border. In fact you could see an American island from where we were standing.

'Well,' I said, 'since this is Canada I'm going to have to call you Caribou Jack. But when you say way up in Canada where do you mean, Caribou Jack?'

'Oh, way up in *northern* Canada.'

'Where? It's a pretty big country you know.'

'Way, *way* up in northern Canada. Almost to James Bay.'

'Oh,' I said. 'You must mean Northern Ontario.'

'Yeah, that's right,' he said out of the corner of his mouth. 'Yeah, I was up there for quite a while. That's where I got the nickname Caribou Jack. They figured I knew more about the wilderness than a native.'

'Really, eh?'

'Yeah. I could smell a caribou or moose or what have you three days after it passed.'

'Three days!' I said. 'Wow!' I spoke softly and looked right at him. He knew he was making a big impression on me. His chest swelled. 'What would a caribou or a moose or what have you smell like, Caribou Jack?'

'Oh that's easy. Just like my wife. That's what it smells like.'

'Don't you like your wife anymore, Caribou Jack?'

'It's like living with a rattlesnake,' he said. 'She's got that bad a bite on her. She's just at me all the time. I can't have any fun when she's along.' He thought a moment. He looked as if he were about to cry. 'I gotta get rid of her.'

'Oh, I bet you say that all the time,' I said.

'No, I don't say that all the time,' he said. 'But I've had enough. Enough's enough. It's true what they say – laugh and the world laughs with you, cry and you cry alone. When I've had enough I've had enough. Yes sir!'

I felt really sad. 'Oh she can't be that bad, Caribou Jack,' I said. 'You've lived with her all these years.'

'Oh yes she is. I took her to Hawaii last year and all the time we were there she wouldn't speak to me. Wasted $2,500. My daughter's coming up on Wednesday or Thursday. I'm hoping she'll take her home with her.'

86
The Knack of Making Friends

I felt a ripple of compassion for Caribou Jack, swamped as he was by waves of jealousy. I tried to make him feel better.

'There's always somebody with a bigger boat than yours,' I said. 'It's true no matter how big your boat is.' He looked thoughtful. I could tell he was taking it in. 'Even your friends with the *million*-dollar boats must feel sick when they see a bigger boat go by.'

He started grinning. 'A friend of mine bought a brand new boat and took it into shallow water and scraped it all up on the rocks,' he said. He certainly had a lot of friends. 'He made a helluva mess of it. The funny thing is, he did it on purpose though. "Now I can have some fun," he said to me.' By this time Caribou Jack was smiling gleefully, his eyes sparkling.

'I wish I had some rich friends like that,' I said. 'It must be the next best thing to being rich yourself.'

'Oh I've got friends everywhere,' said Caribou Jack. 'I have friends among the rich and friends among the poor. Wherever I've gone all through my life I've always had the knack of making friends. Real good friends too. I don't know what it is about me.'

'I can't figure that out either, Caribou Jack,' I said. That was a little mean of me but I knew he wouldn't take it the way it was intended and he didn't. I could tell by the satisfied look on his face. He was squinting out at the lake.

87
Caribou Jack Struggles with His Demon

There were several fishing boats scattered among the islands looming out there across the misty morning waters. The retired school teacher was still sitting in his boat tied to the dock. He seemed to be reading a book. It was probably the instruction manual that came with the boat. Caribou Jack was watching him from a slight elevation where he was warming himself by my fire.

'Another thing about that damn fool boat,' he said. 'It's made of plexiglass. I'd never buy a boat made out of plexiglass. The first rough water it'll fall apart.'

Merle approached us. He'd heard the last part of the discussion. 'That's right,' he said. Merle started telling a story about a guy he knew who drowned in a boat like that while pulling some water skiers. 'The boat just fell apart and the driver flew up in the air and landed in the water. It took them all day to find the body.'

Merle excused himself and walked back to the dock area. Caribou Jack hadn't been listening attentively to Merle's story because he was too busy trying to figure out how he would top it. Since I didn't appear to be going anywhere. He decided to start slowly, sneakily.

'Do you know anything about boat regulations up here in Canada?'

'Nope. Afraid not.'

'I wonder if you need a vent for your motor and gas tank? My youngest son's wife didn't have one on her boat. The whole thing exploded one day. Awful mess. She was no good for a year after.'

'Tsk. That's awful.'

I think Caribou Jack was a little disappointed in my response. I didn't give him a good lead into the next story and he couldn't figure out how to make the transition smoothly. It was as if he were expecting me to say something, as predictable as a chess move, but I wasn't playing properly. We just stood there for a while. Finally he couldn't stand it any more. To hell with transitions — he'd just barge into the next blockbuster of a story.

'You ever fool around on Lake Superior?' he blurted out. 'Boy, they have waves as big as those cottages on that lake. I should know. I lost *five* of my *best* friends on that lake — in one day.'

'No kidding? Wow! How'd that happen, Caribou Jack?'

'There was a storm coming up. You could see it coming. It's easy, don't you know? Whenever I went out fishing my friend and me would take turns watching the weather. First one and then the other. As soon as swells start coming we head in. But this day it was about to storm even before they went out. I told them not to go. But they wouldn't listen. They went out anyway. Then the storm hit. After it was over they still hadn't come in. I knew why not. They were at the bottom of the lake. Two other really good friends of mine went out looking for them — and they never came back either.'

'Seven! Holy God! I thought five was bad enough. But seven of your best friends in one day! Whew!'

Caribou Jack looked pleased. He'd really impressed me, he could tell. He loved the feeling that came with impressing some- **97** one. He decided to hit me with another story, even better if that could be possible. I was a good listener. He'd never let me get away if he could possibly help it.

The next story involved nothing less than a whole ship sinking in Lake Superior, with the loss of about a hundred crew members, although he modestly disclaimed any great friendship with any of them.

It seems Caribou Jack was on an island in the lake and just happened to see the ship go by. And he just happened to tell his friends – a number of his very best friends were there with him – that the ship was going to sink. It was something about the way it was sitting in the water.

And sure enough they heard the next morning the ship had sunk overnight. Caribou Jack wanted to testify at the inquest but nobody would listen to him. 'It was a big cover-up, don't you know?' he said.

88
A Guide Named Beatrice

I could hear stirring inside the van so I told Caribou Jack I wanted to make breakfast for my family. Perhaps I should have invited him to stay. He might have provided some additional stuff for this story. But I was beginning to overdose on him. After a while he made you feel as if *you* were drowning. Even now as I write this I can feel him out there, making friends.

After breakfast we got ready and pulled out. We drove a zigzag route past the bird sanctuary to Fort St. Joseph on the southeastern tip of the island. Or, to be more accurate, the spot where Fort St. Joseph used to be.

Fort St. Joseph was built by the British after the Treaty of Versailles (1783) awarded Fort Michilimackinac to the United States. At the outbreak of the War of 1812 an expedition of traders, British soldiers and Indians set out from Fort St. Joseph, captured Fort Michilimackinac and held it until the end of the war despite intensive American siege and blockade. The Americans were really pissed off. Among other things they burned the vacant Fort St. Joseph to the ground in 1814. It was never rebuilt.

Our guide's name was Beatrice. She met us in the hot, dusty parking lot and we followed her along a footpath leading in a winding manner up over a densely wooded hill, matted with blooming wildflowers. When we got to the top of the hill we saw we were on a kind of peninsula. There was water on all sides, and lots of islands out there to soften storms. A pleasant vista, and a good place for a fort in pre-radar days. You could see the army coming from any direction. No wonder the Americans had to wait until the fort vacated before burning it to the ground. Of course they could have attacked during fog conditions and it would have been a different story. But during fog conditions the Americans might not have been able to find the island. They might have wound up in Tobermory.

Stone buildings were rising dream-like from the earth all around us. It reminded me of my favourite Anglo-Saxon poem, 'The Ruin'. 'Well-wrought this wall; Wierds broke it'. That had been written by an anonymous bard – elegantly meditative and tremendously intelligent – passing by the Roman ruins at Bath in the eighth century. The ruins were about 300 years old at that time – almost twice as old as the ruins here at hand.

University students were digging in the soil under the hot sun. They'd found a gold coin a week or two before but it wasn't available for viewing. It had been sent to Ottawa. Beatrice, under our urging, settled down and began telling us the story of her life. She was tall and thin, freckled and strangely mature despite the braces on her teeth.

She said she'd been born on the island and was studying veterinary science at the University of Guelph. She was going to return to the island and set up practice when she graduated. She was looking forward to being the only vet on the island. So business prospects were excellent. Her father was a teacher at Lakehead College in Thunder Bay.

When we finished the tour Beatrice showed us some sketches of the fort done by artists of the time. She became quite passionate about the poetry of passing time and picked out strange human details in the watercolours and pencil sketches.

We told her about Bruce and his bloody attack on Jennifer. She said she agreed with the vet in the Sault. We told her if we're ever on St. Joseph Island in future years and one of us gets attacked by Bruce we'd be sure to drop in and see her. We told her it would be nice to see her without her braces. She laughed.

Just as we were about to leave she said something strange. 'Maybe being in the United States was driving Bruce crazy'. She had a totally serious look on her face.

'Do you really think dogs are that sensitive to political situations?' I said, nervously.

'Most certainly. Most dogs are more sensitive to things like that than most people', she said. 'But then again for some of the most anti-American Canadians being in the United States is strangely more pleasant than being in Canada'.

'Would that hold for anti-American dogs too?'

'I think so'. I looked at her. She wasn't fooling. 'They can accept   **99**

American culture at its source where it belongs. But it can be very depressing to see it slopping over and greedily sucked up in areas where it simply shouldn't be, at least not in such intensity.'

We walked back down to the parking lot, got in the van and drove off. Except for Beatrice of course. She stayed behind. Strange young woman. And she knew what she wanted to do with the rest of her life. I could see her on that island for the next thirty years, practising animal medicine, specializing in gouging Americans whose pets get car-sick during the summer holidays, then taking glorious two-month winter vacations in Hawaii! Ah, what a life! Clever girl.

89
Graveyard Mushrooms

On the way out we stopped at the old cemetery from the days when the fort was occupied.

I wondered idly how much would be left of them, what their bones would look like now, but decided against getting the shovel from the van and digging them up. Joan and the girls might have got a little sick, just as I probably would get sick if one of them suddenly started displaying such paranormal behaviour. Or would I?

But I did pick some beautiful and edible mushrooms in between the ancient graves.

'Oh no, you're not going to eat graveyard mushrooms,' said Joan.

'Sure. And so will you. And they'll be delicious.'

'I'm not so sure.'

'Oh, come on. Remember Marten Hartwell?'

90
A Picture I Took at That Moment

In front of me as I type is a picture I took at that moment.

Joan was standing at the back of the van with my collection of mushrooms heaped in her arms. The bumper sticker on the van said GOING TO HELL IS BETTER THAN GOING NOWHERE AT ALL. And in the background you can see the old grave markers mouldering away.

'Say cheese,' I said.

'Oh all right. Cheese.'

91
The League of Canadian Poets

The dust was awful that day. When we looked behind as we drove along we could see a huge cloud of dust flying a hundred feet into the air then slowly settling over the mixed woods through which the road cuts.

'This couldn't be doing the woods any good,' I suggested. 'In a couple of years there aren't going to be any trees left.'

'Oh don't be such a worry wart,' said Joan.

92
Haunted by Caribou Jack's Prophetic Powers

So we finally got back on the one paved road, the one that runs a ring around the island, the one the province called Highway 548. But the island people don't call it that. We were driving along the part the island people call the Fifth Side Road. We were heading due west, feeling the land slope down to the shore on our left and slope up to our right to the wooded height of land in the centre of the island.

The paved portion got closer and closer to the shore. Now we were on what the local people called the Huron Line. We looked out over the channel and saw Michigan across the water in one direction and Nebbish Island in another. And further west, Sugar Island. All part of the United States.

Along the shores of the neighbouring islands and the Michigan mainland you could see boathouses and cottages surrounded by immense green foliage, the blue sky and the deep blue shipping channel. It must be a thrilling sight to see a great ocean liner threading through these islands but we weren't lucky that day. Of course we could have waited but who knew how long we would have to wait? Maybe five minutes, maybe a week. Probably not a week. But there was no one to call to find out when a big one was due through.

Suddenly it hit me. This must have been where Caribou Jack was when that fatal ship went through on its way to the bottom of Lake Superior. Remember? The one he predicted was doomed. Something about the way it was sitting in the water. He probably actually did see a ship go by here on its way up to Lake Superior a day or so before that ship went down. And his imagination supplied the rest of the story. Takes one to know one.

93
Enough about Me

We walked around a village known as Sailor's Encampment. The channel between us and Nebbish Island was only about a hundred feet wide. You could almost pick out the dots and dashes of the international boundary glistening in the waves.

And then we were driving north on C. Line towards Richard's Landing, passing by luxurious summer homes owned by Americans, large boats parked in their watery boathouses. Would a boathouse for a houseboat be called a houseboathouse?

In Richard's Landing I sat on a park bench as Joan and the kids visited a crafts store. It was the sort of town where everyone knew everyone else intimately. Where even strangers from out-of-town speak and smile at each other as they pass on the street. Dear hearts and gentle people.

So I sat there on the bench and as people passed I deliberately looked away from them and refused to say anything. I could feel them looking at me, expecting to exchange greetings as befitted the friendly atmosphere. But no, not me. In big cities I'm over-friendly, in small villages underfriendly. But hey, that's enough about me.

Funny how the eastern end of the island was so different from the western. The eastern end was desolate except for fishing camps and the ruins of an old fort. The western end was opulent by contrast with a prosperous-looking town or two, yacht clubs, restaurants, expensive summer homes. It was just like most cities and towns all over Canada: the east end rundown and the west end prosperous. But in this case the reason was more obvi-ous than in most cases. The island's western end was closer to the United States.

94
Greasy Bikers from Minnesota

And there we were, back where we started from at the bridge, wondering what it would have been like if we'd decided to go counterclockwise instead of clockwise. But no, such speculation was idle in the extreme. The whole universe came into being so that Caribou Jack and I could meet that morning. Not to mention Beatrice.

Soon we were driving east on the Trans-Canada Highway again, following the north shore of St. Joseph Channel. In Bruce Mines we stopped for lunch at a place called the Copper Kettle. It was a small restaurant at the back of a gift shop. There were some greasy bikers from Minnesota in there. They were wearing Nazi insignia. They were laughing and as Joan glanced at them two of them happened to glance at her so it looked as if they were laugh-ing at her. At least that's what Joan thought.

'Maybe it was your T-shirt,' I said later. It was a red T-shirt with white lettering. It said on it CENTENNIAL CENTIPEDES and there was a picture of a centipede on it.

'I don't think there's anything funny about my T-shirt,' she said. 'It must have been something else. Do I look funny? Tell me the truth.' She looked at me soberly.

Joan bought some puddingstone which was a geological feature of the area. It's a grey stone with brightly coloured flaws. There's an apocryphal story about some guy from Bruce Mines who travelled all the way to Texas looking for puddingstone around the turn of the century when the mines were getting started. Little did he know that he could have found all he wanted if he'd stayed in his own back yard.

A girl with long luxuriant yellow hair was in charge of the Bruce Mines museum. There was a skull of an Indian woman with a bullet hole in it. I complained to the girl about the use of the term 'squaw' on the card, like a good loyal citizen. She just yawned.

Most of the stuff on display originally belonged to the Cornish miners who came to the area around 1850 to work the copper mines. For instance, there was a fabulous homemade kitchen chair. It had been made over a hundred years ago from one peculiarly shaped branch of a tree. The branch was shaped like this:

and the guy who found it merely sliced it down the middle which gave him both sides of the back and seat and four legs. It was a perfect 'found poem.' If only poets could be that intelligent.

We drove along to Thessalon, along the back streets and down to the waterfront. It was such a *Canadian* town, temporary, unpainted, unplanned. It was so different from the sedate old Europeanesque towns of Southern Ontario, Nova Scotia, or the Eastern Townships. In the park was a plaque commemorating the capture of two American warships in 1814.

On a theatre marquee in Blind River was a sign saying A STAR IS BORN RESTRICTED. 'Aren't we all?' said Joan. Just outside town was a hand-painted sign reading TRAILER STORAGE AVIABLE, available being a word not often heard in ordinary conversation and therefore easily misspelled.

Then in the town of Algoma we passed a guy wearing a grey jumpsuit, all grease-stained. On the back, in what looked like yellow paint, he'd drawn the words BOBO'S DO IT ALL followed by a question mark daubed on as an afterthought. The guy was walking quickly along the street, his shoulders hunched over, his arms swinging in right angles to his direction of travel. I thought of Bob Fones' Bobo stories and decided to check this guy out. I stopped the car and went into a nearby restaurant ostensibly to get a cup of tea for Joan, whom I left sitting in the car with the kids.

As the proprietor prepared the tea in a white styrofoam cup I asked him about Bobo's Do It All.

'The guy with that sign on his back is Bobo,' said the guy. 'He's a real interesting fella. He's been around here for years and years. He lives all by himself in a little trailer outside town and he does odd jobs. He washes windows, rakes lawns and all that. Pretty well any little job you want done, he'll do it. But he doesn't need hardly any money at all to live on because he lives all by himself and that. So with the extra money he gets he buys wheelchairs and gives them to crippled people. So far he's given away nineteen wheelchairs.'

97
Pleasant Moments in a Small-Town Bus Depot

I couldn't get over the atmosphere in that little restaurant. Everyone was so friendly. The place doubled as a bus terminal for the little town and one of the waitresses was filling out a bus ticket for someone who was going to Sudbury. She kept making little mistakes and laughing.

'You should take a coffee break about now,' said the guy buying the ticket.

The bus driver was standing there waiting. 'She's already had six or seven today,' he said.

'It was probably that decaffeinated stuff. What she needs is the real thing,' said the guy.

'That's for sure,' said the bus driver, leeringly.

The girl blushed. She finished off the ticket and handed it to the guy along with his change.

'Geez, I sure don't feel like working today,' said the bus driver as the guy handed him the ticket.

'You don't call driving a bus working, do you?' said the guy.

'Geez, you guys who stay at the Downtowner Inn and get sloshed then figure you can insult the bus driver the next day.'

Just then I went to pick up the tea and managed to hit the edge of the counter with the back of my hand, skinning it in two places. The blood started seeping out. 'Are you insured?' I said to the waitress.

'You just sit down over here and I'll call an ambulance,' she said.

There was an old man waiting for the bus to get going. He was grasping his ticket as if he were afraid he'd lose it. He reminded me so much of my grandfather who died when I was a kid I just had to speak to him for a minute. He seemed so small and feeble.

I'd been thinking of my grandfather anyway because of the great Foreman-Ali fight that had been on television the night before. I'd forgotten all about it until this morning. My grandfather had been a great fan of what he called pugilistics and he used to listen to all the fights on the radio and write about them in his diary. He would write little summaries of the fights just like a real sportswriter. I was only four when he died but I have his diary and I feel as if I knew him. Every time I see a good boxing match on television I think of him and how happy he would have been if he'd lived long enough to see the fights on TV. I don't think he ever went to a boxing match in his life except maybe for some small outdoor bouts at the Hamilton baseball stadium. But he was a hardcore fan and knew about all the famous boxers of the first forty years of this century. This old fellow sitting here reminded me so much of him I asked him if he'd seen the fight.

'What fight?' he said.

'The Foreman-Ali fight last night.'

'Oh yes, I did see it,' he said. 'It was good. Better than wrestling. Wrestling's phoney you know.' He looked at me as if he'd just given me the secret of the universe. As if he almost expected me to disagree.

We continued talking and he pulled out a piece of paper with an address written in a feeble old man's wobbly hand. It said 27 TERRACE STREET. Then under it was the name of a store: PAUL'S LIGHTING FIXTURES.

He asked me if I knew where Terrace Street was in Sudbury. I told him I didn't know. But I told him someone at the Sudbury bus terminal would certainly be able to help him.

He said he had to get to that address to buy some wicks for his son's coal-oil lamps. His son lived in some small town in northern Manitoba. He couldn't remember the name of the town. But it had been hit by a terrible windstorm and the power had been knocked out. His son dug out his old coal-oil lamps to use until the electricity was restored. But he found the wicks had burnt out. So he called his father in Algoma and asked him to pick up some wicks in Sudbury and mail them to him as fast as possible.

'It's an emergency you know,' said the old guy.

I wondered if the son realized how old and feeble his father had become and so I asked the old guy when he'd last seen his son. 'Oh, it's been years and years,' he said.

I later found out there was indeed a Terrace Street in Sudbury, a short alley in the north end, but Paul's Lighting Fixtures had folded years before. I also found out there hadn't been a serious storm in northern Manitoba since the winter. I felt as if I'd stumbled on a real-life Thomas Hardy novel being enacted just outside the range of my peripheral vision.

99
Alison Falls down a Big Hole

'You were gone a long time,' said Joan, sipping her cold tea. So I told her all about Bobo and the old man. Bruce and both kids were sleeping. But they woke up as we got back up to highway speed.

We stopped briefly at Serpent River and walked down the smooth granite shoulders of the fast-moving stream. We were parked next to a van like ours except orange. It had Michigan plates and a bumper sticker that read AMERICA NEEDS YOUR PRAYERS. WILL YOU PRAY? We were parked at the edge of a bluff. I looked down. There was garbage strewn all over the place all the way down. People were taking pictures of the famous Serpent River rapids.

Jennifer came running up to us. 'Alison fell down a big hole,' she said. Our hearts sank like stones and blood drained from our faces.

'I was only kidding,' said Jennifer. 'She's over there.'

'Don't you ever do anything like that again, you hear me?' said Joan.

'Sorry, mommy.'

100
Mild Psychic Torture at Serpent River

I was thinking how nice it was to have Joan and the kids along on this trip. Usually I don't enjoy travelling because of my morbid imagination which pictures all kinds of horrendous things happening to the family at home: Jennifer spilling boiling water all over her pretty little face, Alison being hit by a speeding dump truck, Joan collapsing under the strain of it all without me there to comfort her.

And then climbing up from the river was a little kid blind in one eye. You could see the bottom half of the pupil of his right eye bulging up towards heaven, his other eye as bright as a cat's. He kept running up and down the granite slopes. I shuddered. It was unbearable yet I couldn't take my eyes away from the kid. I noticed a pretty girl about eighteen sitting on a picnic bench with her boyfriend. They were mildly caressing each other. Then I noticed she had only one arm. The right arm ended in a steel hook.

I felt I was being tortured. I found myself muttering to God. I know there's a lot of misery in the world, I said. You don't have to rub my nose in it. Why did God or fate or mathematical chance always push misshaped people into my consciousness like fishermen's hooks? I could remember them all: the midgets, the man with no nose who haunted Kenilworth Avenue all through my childhood and once offered to help me across the busy street to the library, the legless girl who wheeled up to my house one sunny June afternoon in her wheelchair with a stack of handwritten poems she wanted me to read, the spastic who stopped me on the street one day and asked me how I would like to be him. And the dreams, where horribly misshapen and tortured little children approach me and call me Daddy. And the deeper dreams where horrendous monsters with black wings and drooling black pus would rise from the depths of Hamilton Harbour where I was stranded at night in a sailboat with no wind. Why me?

Some sweet violin music was playing on the stereo in Sybil's Pantry, a nice little restaurant in the town of Spanish at the mouth of the Spanish River.

101
Sybil's Pantry

'This is where Frank and Percy and his friends wind up their canoe trip every September,' I said. We were looking at the map. 'See? They bring one van down here to Spanish and load up all their canoes and gear on the other van and take it up here through Sudbury and up to where the Spanish River crosses Highway 144. Then they canoe all the way back down to Spanish. Then they load up the other van and drive back up through Sudbury and along Highway 144 to pick up the second van.'

'Isn't that clever?' said Joan, sarcastically. She doesn't like Frank for several complicated reasons. She doesn't like Percy either come to think of it. It has to do with the way they treat their wives.

There was a nineteenth-century air about this little restaurant. Red velvet wallpaper, English brass rubbings on the wall, framed prints of nineteenth-century landscapes. Even the music, although there'd be no stereo in the nineteen century and a place this small wouldn't be able to support one violinist unless he was playing for his supper.

Sybil was wearing white sandals and a 1940-style dress that came just below the knees. She had a 1940 hair-style and looked as if she should be in uniform. She was constantly laughing at her own jokes and running from the kitchen to the grill to the tables and back to the microwave oven. We were her only customers. It looked as if we might have been the only ones she had all day.

Then she would relax and take long puffs on her cigarette. I was hoping she'd be smoking Players Navy Cut or some other brand from the 1940s like Black Cat Cork Tips, like my mother used to smoke. But they were just Cameos. The kind that hookers generally smoke.

Of course she was English. 'Sybil means witch you know', she said. 'I don't mind if people call me a witch. I think it's true. I am one'. She was just babbling on like that in the most unselfconscious fashion. I loved her.

The kids ordered hamburgers, Joan ordered a schnitzel and I ordered steak and kidney pie. 'We don't have steak and kidney pie today', said Sybil, laughing. She said she was just cooking up a batch of beef and kidneys for the next day.

'Just give it to me without the pastry', I said, feeling like Mr. Leopold Bloom. She said she couldn't do that but offered to mix up some biscuit dough to go with it. It was delicious.

All through the meal Sybil babbled away mostly to Joan. I picked up brief passages of the monologue and then my attention would be distracted by the food. As the meal ended Sybil was telling of the death of her sister in 1943.

Sybil had had a dream three days earlier. She dreamt she was flying over the English countryside and saw an accident. She flew low and followed a speeding ambulance. She saw them pick up her sister's body. Her sister had been riding a motorcycle which was hit by a truck.

'She was only nineteen', said Sybil. 'She was to be married in three weeks'. You could see tears in her eyes. She took another puff on her Cameo.

102
Watching
Television
in Massey

An old guy was sitting down on a chair with his feet propped up on a table just inside the front door of the museum in Massey, Ontario. He was watching a portable television. A commercial for dog food came on. It showed a tiny stagecoach pulled by a team of tiny horses. The stagecoach came out of a dog-food box and sped across the kitchen floor, a full-sized barking beagle in pursuit.

'How do they do that, Dave?' said Joan.

'I don't know'. I looked at the old guy.

'Me neither', he said.

It cost fifty cents to get into the museum but since we'd been in the Bruce Mines museum just down the road we didn't feel like it even though it contained a scale model of the old trading post, Fort Lacloche. We picked up a brochure on Chutes Provincial

Park which was just a little north of Massey. It showed kids in bathing suits sitting on smooth slippery-looking granite rocks bordering a fast-moving stream.

'Want to stay at Chutes tonight?' I said.

'No, it looks too dangerous for Jennifer.'

Joan went back to sit in the car with the kids while I walked down the street looking for a grocery store. I found a little Red and White. When I came out with a bag full of groceries I saw a terrible accident. I think Joan must have had a vague precognitive sense of this accident when she remarked on the park being too dangerous for Jenny. Danger was in the air.

Here it is exactly the way I saw it happen. I walked out of the Red and White store with a bag of groceries. My attention was drawn to two young women walking diagonally across the street. It should be mentioned here that the main street of Massey is the Trans-Canada Highway. The two women were engrossed in a conversation and were paying no heed to traffic. A mail truck came by at about thirty-five miles an hour just as they were about at the centre stripe. The driver honked his horn and a split second later hit the girls. Then he slammed on his brakes and screeched to a stop.

103
An Ordinary Afternoon in Massey

I dropped the bag of groceries and ran out to the girls. They were screaming and moaning. One of the wheels had passed over the leg of the girl closer to me. But there didn't seem to be any serious damage, no bones broken. Just shock. I put my arms around her. 'You're not badly hurt. You'll be fine. Don't worry,' I crooned.

'I'm gonna be sick,' she said, then vomited all over the front of my shirt. She even splattered my face. I don't know what she'd been eating but it just poured out like shit from a cow.

The other girl was in much the same situation – no serious injuries, just shock. But she didn't puke. I helped my girl to the side of the road and some other guy helped the other girl over. The driver of the mail truck just sat behind the wheel. He looked sick too.

Someone asked me if I'd mind directing traffic around the scene of the accident while we waited for the Ontario Provincial Police to arrive. The mail truck had to sit there in the middle of the highway until the official measurements of the skid marks et cetera were taken. So I agreed.

But directing traffic isn't easy. I kept waving traffic on when I should have been signalling it to stop and vice versa. The other guy who was directing traffic further down the street just couldn't get synchronized with me. Then someone else took my place. He was a lot better than me. He talked a lot to the drivers too, or rather shouted.

'What are you waitin' for, Christmas? ... This ain't a peep show ... What's the matter with you? Can't you see a hand signal? ... Come on, get her in high gear ... Let's go ...'

I went back to the sidewalk and picked up my bag of groceries. A big crowd had gathered. They were just standing there watching the girls sitting on the curb crying. Some Indians from the nearby reserve went by but didn't stop. They just kept on walking with hardly a glance at the girls. The girls' parents had arrived on the scene and one of the mothers was near hysterical. 'Would somebody please explain how this happened?' she said. It appeared that I was the only one to witness the accident but I didn't say anything. I was just waiting for the police to arrive to give them my statement. The smell of the vomit was still there but I was getting used to it.

104
A Brain Haemmorhage in Massey

Away up the street I could see our saffron-coloured van parked innocently in the shade of a large small-town roadside maple tree. I expected Joan and the kids to come running down the street, wondering if I'd been hit by a car. But they didn't notice the flashing lights of the ambulance and police cruiser.

The girls were put on stretchers and placed in the ambulance. Nobody complained that it had taken both the ambulance and the police cruiser half-an-hour to reach the scene of the accident.

The police officer was standing amid a good-sized crowd. 'Can anyone tell me what time it happened?' he said.

I was standing off to one side. 'About half-an-hour ago,' I said in a slightly sarcastic tone.

The policeman looked at me. 'I only got the call seven minutes ago,' he said.

The policeman asked me to sit in the back seat of the cruiser next to the driver of the mail truck. His name was Charlie Robillard of Sudbury. He wasn't saying much. I was a little bit mad at him for hitting the girls. He should have seen they weren't going to look. He should have slowed down a lot sooner instead of barrelling through like that.

'It was mostly the girls' fault,' I told the cop as he wrote in his notebook. 'But the driver had a clear view of them. He should

have seen they were engrossed in conversation.'

'I know what you mean,' said the cop. 'You mean he wasn't driving defensively. Right?'

'Right.'

'Well there's probably no criminal charges we can lay. There's nothing in the book about failing to drive defensively. But possibly they'll be able to nail him in civil court. Thanks for waiting, Mr. McFadden.'

As I got out of the car Joan was standing there. She must have noticed the flashing lights after all. 'All right,' she said. 'What happened?'

I told her.

'Oh God,' she said. 'You were gone so long I decided to look back and saw the ambulance. I thought you'd had a brain haemmorhage or something. Oh Christ, I thought. How are we ever going to get home now?'

105
The Girl from Espanola

We threw the groceries in the back of the van and took off out of Massey along the Trans-Canada Highway once again. We were getting close to the point where we'd have to decide whether to head down to Manitoulin Island then take the ferry to Tobermory or continue on to Sudbury and then down the Georgian Bay route. We finally decided on Manitoulin. After all, it's a fabulous place, the world's largest freshwater island and the dwelling place of the good spirit Gitchi-Manitou and his evil counterpart Matchi-Manitou. People have lived there for at least 12,000 years.

We'd all been on Manitoulin Island before but we'd never driven Highway 68 from Espanola to Little Current. It's really the scenic route with a series of hills so rocky and rugged we couldn't believe we were in Ontario.

Espanola is just south of the Trans-Canada. It seemed like a totally ordinary town. There was little to indicate it was a ghost town during the Depression and only revived when the Kalamazoo Vegetable Parchment Company opened a kraft paper mill there in 1945. When I was nineteen I fell in love with a girl from Espanola and was always going to come up here and visit the town and find her but I never did. It would have been inappropriate for me to start looking for her now, with my wife and kids along. If I were alone it'd be a different story.

The rocky hills south of Espanola had been sitting there like that for two and a half billion years. Huge piles of Canadian Shield landstone and granite. And then, with the highway threatening to turn into a roller coaster, there'd be a sudden outcropping of Niagara Escarpment limestone layers crumbling away before our very eyes.

We came out of the hills and onto a plain on the south shore of Birch Island. Across a meadow we could see the tops of two sailboats. It looked as if they were sailing on the grass. And then we crossed the swing bridge into Little Current, the largest and northernmost town on Manitoulin Island.

106
The Four Aces

'I still can't figure out what kitsch means,' said Joan. We were passing a series of Ojibway gift stores along Highway 68 which runs down from Little Current through Sheguiandah and along the shore of Manitowaning Bay. Most of the Indians who live on Manitoulin Island live on the small section of the island east of Highway 68.

'I don't think it really means anything,' I said. Joan had been worried about the word ever since Kay Burkman, a poet from St. Catharines, stayed at our place a while back and complimented Joan on her kitsch decor.

'You've got good taste in kitsch,' said Kay, and Joan didn't want to appear ignorant by asking what is kitsch. But she kept thinking about it, and even went to the library and went through a book of kitsch illustrations trying to figure out what it meant. That didn't help at all.

'It must mean something,' she said.

'As far as I can figure out it's a word used by the upper middle class to describe the taste of the lower middle class. It's a term of condescension. It's a way of dismissing something you don't want to have to deal with, something you don't want to have to take seriously or to pass judgement on. It's something you don't have to take seriously.' I was merely repeating what Greg Curnoe had told me but I wanted to sound original. After all, Joan thinks I'm brilliant.

We came over a hill and there was the place we were destined to spend the night. The Four Aces Campgrounds. It was overlooking Manitowaning Bay, and you could see Winnebagos and tent trailers parked amid the trees. Smoke was snaking its way from tiny bonfires up through the twilight.

At the front was a low white building that housed the office and a small general store for campers and other tourists. Then on the lawn in front of the store were four rectangular pieces of plywood, each about five feet tall and four feet wide, painted and set up to represent the four aces of the card pack. And off to one side were two other large pieces of plywood painted and cut out to represent a dog and a fire hydrant.

'This looks perfect,' said Joan.

107
The Hamilton Tiger-Cats

As we registered I asked the guy about boats. I thought it would be a good idea to take the kids fishing in the morning. When I was a kid my dad and my uncles used to take me fishing a lot. My kids had never gone fishing. The proprietor said the boat and motor would be twelve bucks a day which didn't seem bad. Canoes were three bucks an hour. As for fishing gear, he didn't rent it. 'I've never had any call for it,' he said.

It turned out the guy was a refugee from Hamilton. When he saw me writing Hamilton on the registration form he said, 'How *is* that smokey, polluted city?'

'Terrible,' I said. 'We get away from it every chance we can.' It's simpler than trying to explain why you like it.

'I used to live there,' said the guy. You couldn't really tell by looking at him. 'I was born and raised there.' The guy had a shining bald spot on his head. His wife came up and started smiling. She was about fifty, quite lovely despite the liver spots all over her face.

'Are you from Hamilton too?' I said.

'I was born in Toronto actually,' she said, 'but I lived most of my life in Hamilton.'

'You're smart. You got out.'

'Oh, I don't know. We like it. We still go back quite a bit. Tiger-Cats aren't doing so well this year are they?'

'I wouldn't know. I gave up on that foolishness long ago.'

108
The Energy Crisis

We paid our five dollars and they gave us Number 3. It was supposed to be on the front row so we could watch the sun coming up in the morning over Georgian Bay, if we were up early enough.

But there didn't seem to be a Number 3. There was a camping van with Michigan plates in the Number 2 spot, and another with Ohio plates in the Number 4 spot. The people in Number 2 had sort of spread out along the front of the beach. They had erected two or three tents and a large number of picnic tables and lawn chairs. There was a little pole in front of one of their tents with a rag draped over it. Joan hopped out of the van and lifted the rag. Sure enough. There was a Number 3 under it. So we pulled in, behind the people from Ohio.

Joan was really angry. 'They just put that rag over the pole so nobody would tell them to move.'

'Should we tell them to move over and give us some room?' I said.

'No,' said Joan. 'We'll be leaving first thing in the morning. Let them be.'

We got set up. I plugged in the electrical cord. The outlet was on the same pole. The cord from Number 2 was also plugged in but it didn't fit snugly. It was quite loose. And so was mine. I couldn't get it to fit properly so I changed the two around. That was fine. So I just left it like that.

About an hour later Joan was getting the kids ready for bed and I was sitting at the picnic bench looking at the sky. Some rainclouds were piling up in the west. Then this fat kid about fourteen came over with an unhappy look on his face. He was from Number 2. Bruce came running up to him, wagging his tail. The kid said get away and kicked him. I couldn't believe it.

The kid walked right over to the pole. Apparently their ice was melting. The power had gone off. He looked at the pole and started shouting back at the people at his campsite. I was only about five feet away from him.

'Oh, it figures,' he said. 'They took out our plug and switched it around. They've taken the good one and given us the rotten one.'

I looked at Joan. She was looking out of the van at him. She looked as if she were about to jump out of the van and start beating the kid up. He stormed back to his campsite and whispered something to his father or big brother. Then they got in their pickup truck and drove off with a roar, scattering gravel from the road. I guess they went to complain to the proprietor. I didn't care. I could always insist they move their stuff out of the Number 3 area. But I didn't feel very vindictive. Still, he shouldn't have kicked the friendly little dog.

While he was gone I took a look at the pole. I switched the plugs back the other way. Even though they fit loosely contact was made. 'Have you got power now?' I yelled over to the people from Michigan.

They checked their fridge. 'Yup. It's okay now!'

'Fine then,' I said.

We woke up about two in the morning. The rain was beating on our tin roof. Above the sound of the rain we could hear voices from the next campsite. Actually we couldn't tell where the voices were coming from – the Ohio side or the Michigan side.

There were two men and a woman. The main character had a rich baritone voice like Vaughan Monroe which merely added to the unreality of what he was saying.

'Fuck this, fuck that', he said. 'You fucking bitch. Fuck you.' We could hear him getting to his feet and knocking something over. This went on for quite a while. Joan had to have a pee. The kids were awake and giggling to themselves. Joan started looking through the curtains. The voices seemed to be neither from the Ohio nor the Michigan camp but from a tent across the path – behind us.

The woman's voice: 'You just think you're so fucking smart because you're drinking.' With that Vaughan Monroe let out a yell. It sounded as if he were trying to knock the tent down.

'I didn't ask you', he roared. 'Shut your fucking mouth.'

A few minutes later the spying Joan announced that a couple were behind the tent in a passionate embrace. Meanwhile Vaughan Monroe was inside the tent making himself a tomato sandwich. You could hear him mumbling to himself. He was opening and slamming cupboard doors, slamming down the knife, slamming down the salt shaker. He appeared to be angry because he had to make his own sandwich.

The passionate couple came back into the tent.

'Look, Bob. Don't be so fucking angry all the time you drink.'

'Listen, Arlene. Four months ago I didn't fucking well drink at all.... Want another shot, Jim?'

Things quietened down after that and Joan stole out of the van in her flannel pyjamas. She couldn't hold it back any longer. She squatted behind a tree. Just then a big commotion started again and Vaughan Monroe started screaming that he was going to get into the boat and kill himself. He said he was going to take the boat out a mile or two then put it on full throttle and aim it at the concrete dock.

'Go ahead, then', said Arlene. 'You'd never have enough guts you silly bugger.'

'I wouldn't eh? Well you'll see how much guts I've got. You just wait and see.'

With that, Bob came charging out of his tent and made a wide sweep around our van on his way to the dock. At the same time, Joan was still squatting there behind the tree. As he swept around the tree, Bob almost tripped over her bare bum. 'Oh, excuse me, madam', he said.

'He even smiled,' Joan said when she got back in the van. She giggled.

As we listened a roar from the dock indicated Bob was installed in his death machine and had got the motor going. And vroom off he went in the blackness of Georgian Bay, the motor growing fainter as he went. Soon all we could hear was the rain.

Then the faint sound of the motor floated into our minds again and grew and grew. We lay there wide-eyed in the night as the sound grew dramatically to a roar. We expected at any moment to hear a violent crash as the little boat smashed full speed into the concrete pier. We had a feeling of utter helplessness.

But it didn't happen. At the last minute Bob cut the motor, swerved, and headed back out into the blackness. We realized we weren't the only ones listening. Arlene and Jim were probably sitting there holding hands, wondering if he'd actually do it.

Bob repeated his near miss several times until it got boring and we dropped off to sleep. I'm sorry we can't tell you anything of Bob's fate because we just don't know. That's the nature of this sort of book, unfortunately. And of course of this sort of life.

We pulled out of the Four Aces fairly early in the morning, before the others began stirring. We wanted to get to South Baymouth before 9:10 when the ferry was due to leave for Tobermory.

111
A Ferry Tale

It was still raining. That's why we were in a hurry to take the morning ferry. Manitoulin Island is gloomy in the rain.

'I don't like camping any more,' said Joan. 'I want to sell the van.'

I noticed she no longer called it Gus. When we first got the van we always called it Gus the Bus, after Gus McFarlane our big fat Member of Parliament.

We arrived at South Baymouth with plenty of time to spare. Ten minutes in fact. We were the second car in the line-up. But the line-up wasn't moving. Then I realized why. The ferry was already filled to capacity. I walked up to the car ahead of us. It was an MG with Manitoba plates. A guy with a walkie-talkie and a blue uniform was measuring it with a tape measure. 'Okay, go ahead,' he said.

Then he measured our van. 'Thirteen feet,' he said over the walkie-talkie.

Back came the answer: 'No, he's about two inches too long.'

'That's it,' said the guy with the tape. 'You're going to have to wait for the one-thirty ferry.'

'One-thirty! It's only nine o'clock. Oh Christ!'

Just then the ferry started pulling out, a huge boat filled with hundreds of cars, Winnebagos, buses, tractor trailers, motorcycles, bicycles, everything. The gulls were squealing with delight in the morning rain, and travellers were standing on the wet decks taking wet pictures of the wet loading docks.

I was infuriated. It looked as if they were taking pictures of my van, the only vehicle not able to get aboard. I jumped out and ran to the edge of the dock then began shouting and making a fist at the ferry.

'Goddamn it, it's all these Goddamn Americans with their Jesus big Winnebagos', I yelled. I was really mad. One of the tourists on the boat shook his fist back at me then snapped my picture.

A rope was dangling from the end of the boat as it moved out into Lake Huron. 'Look kids', I said. 'A ferry tail.'

112
Scrambled Eggs

We sat in silent gloom in the van for an hour while the rain stopped and more vehicles pulled up to join us in our long wait for the afternoon ferry. Finally we decided it was time for breakfast. The four of us walked across the broad expanse of the parking lot to the restaurant, a large frame building. It looked as if it had been converted from a house. It was called the Ferry Diner.

It was cafeteria style and there were several people sitting at tables stuffing themselves with scrambled eggs. Behind the cafeteria counter was a big chalked sign reading BREAKFAST MENU. We stood there reading it.

SCRAMBLED EGGS

BACON   HAM   OR SAUSAGES

TOAST   COFFEE $2.50

TOAST JAM COFFEE .90

CORN FLAKES .75

Next to it was another large chalkboard sign spelling out a sad fact of civilized life:

WASHROOMS FOR CUSTOMERS ONLY

I walked up to the girl behind the counter. 'What about fried eggs or poached eggs?'

'We only have scrambled eggs', she said as if it were extremely rude of me to ask.

'But we like our eggs fried. Is there another restaurant around?'

The girl broke into a smile. 'No', she said.

Joan almost hit the roof. 'Come on, Dave. Let's go', she said. 'I wouldn't eat here if I was starving.'

113

**The Secretary
of Lakehead
University**

All around us gulls were squealing with unearthly delight. At the dock two kids were fishing for perch. They caught several little ones. We let Bruce run for a minute and he chased about 144 gulls off the dock.

Joan started preparing breakfast in the van. Fried eggs and bacon, coffee, toast. Everything. A guy who looked like a real estate agent and his wife were sitting in a brand new grey Lincoln parked next to us. They gave us occasional snooty looks.

'I'm not the slightest bit embarrassed', said Joan. 'Let them pay $2.50 for breakfast and make those slimey crooks rich'.

After breakfast, which was delicious, I started writing in my book. Joan became alarmed.

'This is the only restaurant around here. People will know which one you're talking about. You're going to get in trouble'.

'Oh Joan, haven't you ever heard of fair comment? Besides, I didn't use the restaurant's real name. It's really called the Summer Kitchen'.

The kids picked up Joan's unease. 'I hope this book never gets published', said Jenny.

'Don't say anything', said Alison. 'Daddy'll write it down'.

There was a little kid about five running around with a war bonnet on his head complete with eagle feathers. He also had a little Indian drum and a stick. It looked as if he'd been outfitted in one of the Indian craft stores on the island.

'This whole thing is making me sick', said Joan.

'I thought you'd feel better after breakfast. Want some more tea?'

'I'll get it myself. And that big fat kid from the States who kicked Bruce. I'd like to punch the shit out of him. Little Brucie wagging his tail for a little attention. *Get away!* Poor Brucie just walked away with an awfully hurt expression on his face'.

I got out and watched the two kids fishing. They caught several more little perch and put them on a string. They'd make a fabulous lunch.

A guy from Timmins came by and began chatting. I asked him what were his favourite fish. He said he liked pickerel best. I told him I liked whitefish and trout.

'That too', he said. The kids seemed worried we were going to steal their fish.

Along came a guy in leather shorts, German style. What do they call them? Liederhosen? We got talking and it turned out he was the secretary of Lakehead University. He had come all the

118

way from Thunder Bay along the south shore of Lake Superior. 'It's even more scenic than the north shore', he said. He began telling us some funny stories about moose hunting. Then he told a good story about Irving Layton, a Canadian poet of the 1950s. I'd repeat the story if I could remember it. All I can remember is it involved Irving's famous ego. At any rate the guy seemed to remember Layton with affection. I told him Layton always reminded me of Wilson MacDonald, a poet from Port Dover, who also considered himself the greatest poet who ever lived.

'It's probably a tie', he said.

We were aboard the *Chi-Cheemaun*. It was only about its second year of operation and it was a nice boat. The seagulls were flying at exactly the same speed. A guy with a bag of Cheezies was standing on the outer deck feeding the little orange things to the gulls. He would hold a Cheezie between his forefinger and thumb. The bird would fly up and, still flapping its wings to maintain the same speed as the boat, would put its bill carefully around the Cheezie and swoop away with it as if it were a little goldfish. The guy then looked through the window into the inner decks to see if anyone was watching.

I remembered the last time we were on this ferry I saw an Amish farmer doing the same thing, but with more gusto somehow, and less self-consciousness. As the gull flew up and took the Cheezie, the farmer laughed with glee and at no time did he look to see if anyone was watching him. Of course everyone was. It was beautiful to see a totally natural man.

By the way, he was wearing suspenders *and* a belt. I can remember about thirty years ago my father being amused by some old guy who was wearing suspenders and a belt. 'That's known as hedging your bets', he said.

It was also strange that the Amish farmer was using Cheezies as well. Maybe it's a tradition on this boat to feed Cheezies to the gulls. Almost everything we do we have seen someone else do before. I must be getting old. It reminds me that I probably know a poet who knew a poet who knew a poet (and so on and so on) who knew Homer. All the way back. Every word a step in the darkness.

114
The Poet Who Knew Homer

I was standing on the deck of the *Chi-Cheemaun*, right in the bow. The wind was blowing in my face so hard I had trouble breathing. I was watching the small rocky wooded islands pass us on either

115

A Typical Conversation between Two American Tourists

side. As we pushed forward the islands seemed to revolve like saucers on the ends of sticks. You know that juggler who always used to appear on the Ed Sullivan Show in the 1950s spinning plates on the ends of sticks?

There was an interesting conversation going on behind me. I didn't bother looking back at the men talking so I can't describe them at all. But they had Midwest American accents. Here is the conversation as I heard it:

'I've got a big '73 Chrysler New Yorker.'

'So have I.'

'We left Sault Ste. Marie this morning.'

'So did I.'

'We had breakfast in a nice little restaurant in a place called, uh, Bruce Mines.'

'The Copper Kettle?'

'That's it.'

'So did I.'

'We're going to take in that theatre at Stratford. *Richard III* and *As You Like It*. I like it myself.'

'I like it myself too.'

'My son graduated from college and there was nothing in his field so he went to law school.'

'So did mine.'

And on and on like that.

116

Ezra Pound and Ernest Hemingway

I would have listened to this fascinating conversation for a lot longer but it was too cold out there on the outer deck. It was summer and I was wearing a jacket but the jacket was too thin for the cold Lake Huron breeze.

So I went back in the tourist compartment. Joan was sitting on a bench facing two elderly women with blue hair. They'd discovered Joan was a school teacher and since they were retired school teachers themselves they had lots to talk about. They were talking about all the travelling they'd done since they'd retired.

'We've been just everywhere,' they said, delightedly. I decided to play a joke on them.

'Have you been to Mount Hope?'

'Mount Hope? Where's that?' they said, suspiciously.

'It's about four miles south of Hamilton on Highway 6.'

'Well no. We haven't actually been *every*where.'

They didn't seem to think that was much of a joke. A sense of humour was missing from their lives. Maybe that's why they were living such long healthy lives. Laughter can be harmful to your health. I can't remember where they were from. I can remember *them* well but not where they were from. Funny because for me that's usually the most important thing about a person.

But we talked for quite a while and I found out about some islands off the coast of Georgia, and Kauai, one of the Hawaiian islands. It was just like reading the *National Geographic*.

When I was a kid I always used to read *National Geographic* magazines at the Kenilworth branch of the Hamilton public library because we couldn't afford a subscription at home. The Hamilton Spectator was all we could afford. There was a whole room on the second floor devoted to old copies of the *National Geographic* going back to 1888. The library was a nineteenth-century cottage and there was a fireplace in the room. I loved it.

So every week when we had to do a book review I'd always review some back issues of the *National Geographic*.

One day the teacher, apparently after some serious deliberation, wanted to talk to me about my book reviews.

'Do you read each issue you review from cover to cover?'

'Yes', I said. I think I was lying.

'Even the ads?'

'Well, no.'

'Then I think you'd better review real books rather than magazines from now on if you don't mind. I think that would be a lot better. Don't you?'

'Yes, Miss Addleton.'

It was good she did that. If it weren't for her I never would have read *For Whom the Bell Tolls*. Or Pound's *Cantos*. And then I wouldn't have grown up to be such a fabulous writer, at least as good as Irving Layton and Wilson MacDonald. Certainly a *lot* better than Ralph Gustafson.

Funny the way things remind you of things. The two retired school teachers reminded me of Miss Addleton and they also reminded me of the *National Geographic* which also reminded me of Miss Addleton. And Miss Addleton reminded me of Ernest Hemingway and Ezra Pound.

As far as writers are concerned, a lot of writers might also have forgotten – as did I – where those two elderly women came from but they probably wouldn't have admitted it and would have made up some place. Like Paris, Ontario, or London, Ontario, or Shakespeare, Saskatchewan. But not me. I'm too honest. You can put your trust in David McFadden.

By the way, Ezra Pound was always Ernest Hemingway's big

hero. He never hesitated to acknowledge that fact. Pound could do no wrong as far as Hemingway was concerned. And never did. Pound of course scarcely knew Hemingway existed.

Further, we always hear of how Pound helped James Joyce among others. But I have a theory that Hemingway did more than anyone else to help Joyce, although it was in a totally indirect manner. Joyce came out with *The Dubliners*. Hemingway read it and stole the style lock, stock and barrel. When Hemingway became famous Joyce couldn't continue writing in his own voice because Hemingway had appropriated it. So he had to move on into other voices. Without Hemingway's larceny there never would have been a need for a *Ulysses* or *Finnegans Wake*. There just would have been a lot more fiction in *The Dubliners* style. Joyce would have had to write *The Sun Also Rises*.

117
Ballast Stones

Joan began to tire of the women so we excused ourselves and went into the cafeteria. There was a line-up. It took a good five minutes before I reached the cash register. There was a little red heart stuck to it. Then I discovered I had nothing smaller than a twenty-dollar bill and the girl behind the cash register was short of change.

The guy behind me was very nice about it. He pulled out his wallet. 'Can I help you?' he said. 'You're in the yellow van, aren't you?' He gave me three dollars. 'Take this and you can pay me back later, maybe when we dock.'

So I paid for the two pots of tea and one Danish. When I got back to the table Joan looked at the Danish and said she wanted one too. So I went back to the cashier and asked for another Danish. I still had some change left from the three bucks.

Strange coincidence. The guy in front of me this time also only had a twenty. But finally the guy found some change in a pocket he didn't know he had, like in those dreams when you're in your own familiar house and you suddenly discover a room you never before knew was there. And if you're brave enough to enter the room you'll find a priceless treasure.

When the guy had gone the cashier took my money. There was no one behind me so we chatted for a minute. 'Maybe I could ask the captain to put in at one of those islands,' she said, 'so you could get some change.' She was younger than me but she seemed to be taking a maternal interest. It made me feel a little shy.

'No. Don't bother doing that for me,' I said. 'I'm nobody important.'

'Really?' she said, teasingly. 'I could have sworn you were some-one *very* important. 'You're not in the movies are you? Or in the arts in some way?'

'Why yes as a matter of fact I am', I said. 'In the arts I mean.'

'Oh really. I thought so', she said. 'Now let me see. Who would you be? I know you from somewhere. Give me a hint. What branch of the arts are you in?'

'The martial arts', I said. 'I take kung fu lessons at the Y.'

'Mm. Interesting. I bet you're involved in other arts as well?'

This was getting ridiculous. Did I look arty? Should I tell her I'm quite interested in the art of love? Nah, not with my beloved wife right over there waiting for me to return with the Danish.

'None that I can think of off-hand. None that I'd like to tell you about anyway. Just kung fu', I said. 'But it wouldn't do for the captain to pull in at one of these islands even if he wanted to.'

'Why not?'

'They're all uninhabited, aren't they? There'd be no one on them with any change.'

'No. But some of them allow overnight camping. And you know if there's overnight camping allowed there has to be a laundromat, with coin-operated machines. And if there's coin-operated machines there has to be a change-making machine. Oh wait a minute. I lie. Cove Island is inhabited. They have a light-house there and I'm sure the operator would have some change. Are you interested in old lighthouses?'

'Sure. Isn't everybody?'

She ignored the question. 'There's a really old one on Cove Island. It was built in the early part of the nineteenth century.'

'Really, eh? How early?'

'Oh, about 1880.'

'What? That's not early.'

'It's earlier than 1890.'

I couldn't believe this conversation. The girl looked a lot like Jeannie Wyatt but she'd be about ten years younger. I used to have insane conversations like this with Jeannie Wyatt in high school.

She started talking about how the early lighthouses on the Great Lakes were built out of ballast stones which ships carried after they dropped their cargo and had nothing else to pick up. I took the Danish back to Joan.

'You were gone a long time', said Joan.

'Oh. Don't you know what happened?'

118

A Black Woman in a White Cadillac

'No. What?'

'Someone fell overboard. That little self-conscious guy who was feeding the gulls? He just reached over too far and fell in. It looked like one of the gulls did it on purpose by holding back a bit. Anyway I had to jump in after him and save his life.'

'Get off it.' You couldn't fool Joan. 'Your clothes aren't even wet.'

'No. The captain pulled in at one of the islands and I threw my clothes in a coin-operated dryer. Didn't you hear the engines slow down and stop?'

'No. I was too engrossed in my thoughts.'

'What were you thinking about?'

'I'm not telling *you*.'

'Well, that's what happened.'

'I believe you.'

'You do? You believe that? That was just a cover-up. What really happened was I went down to the vehicle level and made love with a beautiful black woman in the back seat of her white Cadillac. She was just like Billie Holliday.'

'It's not fair to tell lies.'

119

How to Seduce Black Women

I feel sad today. The book-banners are out in force. There's even a town in Ontario where they're trying to ban *Who Has Seen the Wind*. And every time I flick on the television all I see is a panel of dopey-looking American evangelists.

A guy waving a Bible got up in a meeting in a school gym in Clinton, Ontario, a few days ago and said, 'All the English literature anyone needs is right in this book.' He wasn't molested.

It appears these stupid anti-life people want to ban literature entirely, perhaps because they're too dumb to see anything in it and it merely stands to remind them of their low intelligence levels. But the time is not yet right for that. So for now all they can do is ban books that contain the word 'fuck.' As far as this book is concerned, if the title of this chapter has attracted any potential book-banners, I heartily entreat them to ban this book. *A Trip around Lake Huron* is a perverse, scurrilous book. The author wants to corrupt your kids. At least he doesn't want them to grow up to be mean, crabby bastards like you.

Imagine! This book was funded by the Canada Council and contains a chapter entitled 'How to Seduce Black Women.' And to make things even worse it has nothing to do with seducing black women. All it talks about is the attempted seduction of Canadian children by book banners who want to bring back slavery.

The *Chi-Cheemaun* docked in Tobermory and suddenly the town of Tobermory doubled its population. I looked around for the guy who loaned me the three bucks but couldn't find him. I guess he had forgotten. God bless you, wherever you are. You have true generosity of spirit. I'd be surprised if *you* were involved in banning books.

We parked in downtown Tobermory and sat on a public bench in the sun. It was nice. And oh, the boats in Tobermory Harbour! This seemed to be some kind of centre for the ostentatious wealthy from all around the Great Lakes. And it's easy to see why. The water is so deep and clear and there are so many thousands of uninhabited islands to explore within a few hours' sailing.

Members of the Boy Scout troop from Mount Olive, Indiana, were wandering all around the town in their olive-coloured uniforms covered with badges. Jennifer and I strolled out on the dock to take a close look at *The Firefly* from New York City. I wondered if it came up through the Gulf of St. Lawrence or the Erie Canal. I thought of Caribou Jack's friends and their million-dollar boats. Jennifer held my hand. I felt sort of inadequate. For a moment it seemed the ultimate human tragedy that a beautiful child like Jennifer should have a father like me who can't even afford to take her sailing in the Great Lakes. She deserved better than me.

No one seemed to be home in *The Firefly* but there was someone stirring aboard *The Lady* from Troy, Michigan, which was moored right beside it.

'Would you like to have a boat like this some day, Jennifer?' I said.

'Yeah,' said Jenny. 'But it would cost too much money.'

'Maybe you'll be rich some day.' I felt like getting down on my knees and begging forgiveness for not having made more of my talents, for not having used my fine mind to amass a fortune for her rather than write these useless books.

Just then someone came out of the cabin. It was a girl about eighteen with a horsey face. She tilted her head back and looked at us along her long nose, a natural look of superiority. She looked as if she expected us to be embarrassed at finding out someone had been in there listening to us. She looked as if we'd said something to offend her. I wondered what she'd heard of our little conversation, and what she'd thought she'd heard.

All she said was 'humph.' Then she turned her back, ducked and went back into the cabin.

121
I Get to Talk to a Rich Man

We stood there a minute longer looking at the boats. I guess we were making some of the people feel a little nervous. Maybe they thought we were trying to look through portholes at them. But surely they'd be resigned to being gawked at when they entered harbour.

A man about fifty came out of the *Phoenix III* from Beverly Shores, Indiana.

'Are you the harbourmaster?' he said. There might have been a slight sarcastic tone in his voice. I told him no. 'Too bad,' he said. 'You could have collected a lot of money.'

'I'm too honest for that,' I said. He just looked at me, wondering if *I* were being sarcastic.

'Which is your vessel?' Vessel? Why didn't he just say boat? And why did he assume I had a boat?

'The yellow one over there.' He looked. I pointed at the van.

'Oh. Heh.'

'Heh.'

122
The Purple Moose

We were happy as all get out because it was only a few miles from Tobermory to our favourite place in the whole world: Cypress Lake Provincial Park. After a couple of hours wandering around Tobermory we no longer could postpone our bliss. We got in the van and took off along Highway 6 which, if we kept on it long enough, would pass right by our house in Hamilton.

But after a few minutes we hung a left and began driving down a narrow winding road through the cedar forest towards the edge of the Niagara Escarpment and glorious Georgian Bay. Our hearts were pounding.

Nothing could take away our love for Cypress Lake, not even the misery of our visit last fall. It was early fall and we weren't prepared for such cold, rainy weather. But even worse than the weather were the people we were with. Mind you, they're very nice people and I like them a lot. But they're no fun to go camping with.

You see, Luella and Simon are health-food proponents and teachers of yoga and meditation. Don't ever go camping with health-food proponents and teachers of yoga and meditation unless you're a health-food proponent and teacher of yoga and meditation yourself.

There was Joan frying eggs over the sputtering campfire under an almost-black mid-morning sky. She was wrapped in my hydro parka. Luella reached over and cracked one of her own eggs into a bare spot in the pan. Her upper lip wiggled with glee. 'Oh look everybody', she said. 'Look at my organic egg beside Joan's ordinary eggs. Mine makes hers look *sick*. Mine's so much bigger and the yolk is a darker orange.'

I was pleasantly surprised that Joan didn't shove the eggs frying pan and all down Luella's throat. In fact it might have been a lot better if she had. After breakfast Joan started doing the dishes. 'Oh, use my soap, Joan', said Luella. 'Mine's bio-degradable.'

We'd been eagerly anticipating a fabulous weekend but it didn't turn out that way. We certainly didn't mind foregoing meat. Joan isn't much of a meat-eater anyway. And it was nice to take a holiday from the kids.

But we did take Bruce along much to Luella and Simon's annoyance. Bruce would bark a little whenever a chipmunk or groundhog would pass by, and it was getting on their nerves despite the fact that they were yoga and meditation teachers. And the blue jays. Joan and I were in ecstasy over the blue jays, they were so beautiful. But Luella and Simon would moan and cover their ears with distaste whenever one would screech. They called them garbage birds. They made us feel we were stupid because we *liked* blue jays.

All four of us went for a long walk that afternoon, scrambling down the limestone cliffs of the Niagara Escarpment to the cold blue waters of Georgian Bay. At one point I fell off a rock and hurt my thumb. Luella applied Rescue Ointment, a homeopathic remedy with brandy and assorted secret organic compounds, and it felt better. I took off my shirt and shoes and dived into the water with just my jeans on. It was incredibly cold. The next thing I knew Luella had taken off her jeans and was swimming beside me in her panties and transparent blouse. She threw her arms around me and shivered with delight. I looked up at the high rocks and there was Joan standing there fuming, hands on hips.

That was the night of the big Canada-Russia hockey game and I wanted to go into town to watch it but they wouldn't let me go because they didn't want to sit in a smokey pub with beer-drinkers. But at 7:30, just before the game was due to start, they had a change of heart. They decided we'd go to Tobermory to get some special candy that's made there. The candy store was closed though so we ended up at the only hotel in town – the Tobermory Lodge – and had ice cream sundaes, chocolate milk and cherry cheesecake. You should have seen them wolfing down all this health food! I asked the guy running the place where his TV was. **127**

He said he didn't have one. 'This is a high-class place,' he said. Honest.

The next day John and Janet Boyle came up from Owen Sound. They brought their yellow canoe with the purple moose painted on the side – a purple moose being John's trademark as a famous Canadian painter.

'Did you paint that moose yourself, John?' I said. It didn't quite look his style.

'No,' said Janet. 'He had it painted. He can't paint that good.'

The Boyles are Canadian wine afficianados and brought along a bottle of Canadian Tawny Port. The four of us drank it while Luella and Simon looked on coldly and sipped unfermented, unpasteurized apple juice with no additives. The Boyles refused to eat any of Luella's food. Janet had brought bologna and cheese sandwiches.

Simon took me to one side. 'He can't be a good artist if he eats like that,' he said.

'Well he is,' I said. 'It takes more than meditation and bean sprouts to be an artist.' Simon winced. He paints a bit.

Anyway the Boyles brought too much food and wound up feeding some of the bologna to Bruce. 'Here,' said Simon. 'Feed him this cheese too. It's pasteurized. And the bread. It's store bought, full of chemicals.' Poor Bruce almost got poisoned.

It was an awful experience. I particularly felt sorry for John and Janet although we had a good canoe trip Sunday afternoon. Janet was several times on the verge of smashing Luella's face in with a rock.

Luella and Simon were totally exhausted at the end of the weekend while Joan and I were more refreshed than when we arrived. Luella was complaining of headaches, stomach aches, running nose, hypoglycemia, tiredness, general allergies and low blood sugar. They even had more mosquito bites than we did. In fact we didn't have any.

And best of all, Luella and Simon came equipped with Kodiak Grebs, which are supposed to be the ultimate in walking shoes. Joan and I had our ordinary loafers. Yet we were the ones who had to show *them* how to walk gently and avoid blisters. Their feet were destroyed by the time we packed up Sunday night.

'Even if I'd been half-dead I wouldn't have let on,' said Joan.

But now it was another year, the warm sun was shining, and we were again driving down the narrow road to the park. The woods were carpeted with a magic display of wild mushrooms. Joan was giving some editorial comment on the news of Luella

and Simon's split-up a few weeks earlier.

'You told me I was just jealous last fall when I told you they wouldn't be together a year from now. But I was right wasn't I?'

'Ah, she probably told you she was going to dump him.'

'No she didn't. Not her. I could just tell. I'm smarter than you think.'

After we got settled I went to the toilet and saw this strange bit of pathos scrawled on the wall:

I AM 6'4" 221 lbs
and scored 3 TDs in the 1971
ROSE BOWL
100 yards 9.7 secs
Bench Press 420 lbs
and didn't get drafted by any
pro team!   Bastards!

And it was signed Elwood Washington. Under it someone had written 'American bullshit.'

What increased the strangeness of the message was its location, far from the world of commerce. We were surrounded by dense forests, misty lakes, mystical limestone caverns, the mysterious Niagara Escarpment and deep pure blue Georgian Bay. To quote from a story on the Bruce Peninsula that appeared in *Scenic Wonders of Canada*: 'The forest floor is made up of limestone slabs four and five feet across. Between them are cracks a few inches wide, deep and filled with rich soil that has a springy carpet of moss and is topped by a variety of wild flowers in spring and summer. Bird's-eye primula, dwarf iris and marsh marigolds spring into bloom in May. The colours of Indian paintbrush, blue-eyed grass and twinflower are added in June. By July the bladderwort and rare ferns such as hart's-tongue fern, wall rue fern and walking fern cautiously emerge for their brief season in the sun, along with several varieties of wild orchids ...'

I thought I'd check out Elwood Washington. A few days after we got home I phoned the Canadian Football League head office. The secretary-treasurer said no one by that name had ever tried out for any pro team in Canada. Next I checked out the 1971 Rose Bowl. He could have been referring to the one played Jan. 1, 1971, or Jan. 1, 1972, so I checked both. I went to the newspaper office and checked the microfilms for those days. No one by the name of Elwood Washington was mentioned in either.

124
Canadians Aren't as Smart as Americans

On another wall someone had written something less literate but more poetic perhaps:

> Shite House Poits
> Wane thy Day
> go to THE SHITE HOUSE
> in the SKY
>
> in th way over
> they will ride
> SHITE MOUNTS
> to the SKY

When you see writing on the toilet wall, unless there is specific reference to nationality, one can only assume the writer is a native of the country in which the toilet is located. Tourists are more over-bearing and boastful, while locals are less pretentious, and are somewhat absent-minded, repetitive and unselfconscious. Locals are also occasionally political as on the walls of public toilets at rest stops along the Trans-Canada Highway in Quebec where there are many anti-tourist and anti-anglais slogans simply because the writers know a lot of tourists and anglais use these particular toilets. A captive audience.

By this token Elwood Washington, whom we can assume was an American, seemed much more skilled in language, spelling and grammar than the anonymous Shite Mounts Poit. And although I generally speaking dislike generalities one could be forgiven for deducing from these two examples and others like them that Americans are by and large more intelligent than Canadians. Of course the Shite Mounts Poit showed a lot more vision and imagination than Elwood Washington, but that's another story.

You may think I'm hanging my conclusion on very slim threads. But just a few moments after stepping out of that washroom I observed a little tableau that, as far as I'm concerned, proves my point.

I was walking along the dirt road on my way back to the camp. In front of me I couldn't help noticing a very attractive collie on a leash being held by a young woman in the briefest of bikinis. There were signs all over the park reading DOGS MUST BE KEPT ON LEASH. Oh well, it could be worse. It could be *Jews* or *Niggers* or *Poets* or *Zen Buddhists* or even *Americans* MUST BE KEPT ON LEASH. You have to draw the line somewhere. And I'm no racist although some of my best friends are. I try to tell them but they

130

just laugh at me and say ah come on, don't be so serious. Have a drink, Dave. And then I'd start to smile and everything would be okay. We'd get out the old chequerboard and have two or three games then go down to the corner and shoot some pool or maybe bowl a few games.

Anyway, a couple of young fellows in a souped-up hotrod, 1955-style, chopped and channelled with fender skirts, a Continental Kit and Hollywood mufflers, passed me on the road then pulled up alongside the girl and her dog. I couldn't hear what they were saying at first so, without trying to attract attention, I walked a little more quickly and tried to get within earshot. Just for the book of course.

'Ah come on, baby. Why don't you come to town with us and have a few drinks and maybe dance a little and who knows what else, eh? It's going to be a pretty boring night.'

By the way the girl and her dog were walking I could tell the girl didn't know these men and wasn't particularly appreciative of their attention. She kept slowing down, drawing back and then the car would slow its pace and wait for her. Then she would start walking fast and the car would speed up a bit to keep even with her.

Then finally I guess the guys got tired of pleading for suddenly they gunned the motor and sped away, tossing little pebbles and chunks of earth all over the road.

When everything went quiet again the woman stopped, knelt down, and began scratching her dog's ears. 'Never mind, Bobby,' she said. 'They were only Canadians.' The dog looked about ten years old so it was probably born around the time of the assassination of US Senator Bobby Kennedy.

I didn't want to make myself obvious by stopping when the woman stopped so I kept on going right past her as she knelt there scratching the dog's ears. I might have made some kind of friendly remark in passing but since she was an American I felt sort of self-conscious. She might have looked up at me curiously as I walked by but I don't know for sure because I didn't look down.

Just as I was typing the previous paragraph the phone rang. I tend to fluctuate wildly in my expectations about the work in progress. At that moment I was thinking that the book was going to be a smash hit and I'd become a genuine Canadian hero, or maybe even a bogus one. Then the phone rang and I picked it up. A female voice said: 'Hello? Is this Dr. Bethune?'

'Uh, pardon?'

'Is this Dr. Bethune's office?'

'Uh no, it's not. Definitely not. You must have the wrong number.'

'Oh I'm sorry. Stupid of me.'

'By the way, would that be Dr. *Norman* Bethune?'

'Well, I'm not sure of his first name. Why? Do you think you know him?'

'Well yes. But this definitely is the wrong number.'

'Okay, thank you.'

Sorry for that little break in the narrative. To get back to the American girl in the bikini, what more can I say except to say she didn't invent the supposition she implied in her singular remark. It was something she was born with, something that is part of the communal mind, the global mind. Canadians believe it, Americans believe it, the English believe it, probably the Tibetans and the Vietnamese believe it too. The writing's on the wall. Canadians aren't as smart as Americans.

125
A Normal Dream of the Late Twentieth Century

That night I had a nightmare. Joan and I were locked in a room. There was one window facing into another room. The rooms were something like cells in a prison. A beautiful young couple in their early twenties were taken into the next room and tortured. We could see them through the window screaming in agony. It was awful.

We couldn't see their torturers. We couldn't clearly see how they were being tortured. But we could clearly see the intensity of their agony. Their screams were unbearable. They were being kept just below the passing-out level. They were experiencing the ultimate extremes of pain and we were totally helpless. All we could do was watch.

Then I noticed Joan couldn't take it any longer. Her face was losing its normal muscle tone. She began talking nonsense, baby talk. The horror of what we were witnessing had destroyed her mind. I felt my own mind starting to go. Then I woke up.

126
Gerry Gilbert

The next day the trees were full of blue jays and chipmunks. It was just like being part of nature. I collected some interesting mushrooms and was trying to identify them. It was difficult.

I thought I had some beautiful worm-free specimens of *Boletus edulis* which in Europe are prized to the extent that mushroom lovers charter trains to go into the forests on collecting trips when the mushroom is in season. But when I cooked them up and tasted them they were terrible. So maybe I was mistaken.

A lot of the mushrooms, especially the boletus, came with transparent slugs sleeping in hollowed-out tunnels in the flesh. They reminded me of the poet Gerry Gilbert on the other side of the continent. His trademark is the slug and he carries one with him in a matchbox.

It was amazing how few mushrooms I could identify. Most of them were in the grey zones *between* something and something else. It was humiliating. Every time a new mushroom field guide comes out, it seems another thousand varieties of mushrooms have evolved.

I took a walk around Cypress Lake marvelling at the variety of mushrooms. It was like skindiving in a tropical sea swarming with brightly coloured aquatic life. The mushroom I loved most was the *Amanita frostiana.*

I brought about twelve of them back to the camp. They were each about two-and-a-half inches long, their yellow caps changing to bright orange at the centre and flecked with little white warts. They closely resembled the fabled *Amanita muscaria* but they were smaller, their stems were thinner and touched with yellow instead of being completely white, and the volva formed a little white boot with a free collar at the margin unlike both the *A. muscaria* and *A. flavoconia.*

It was definitely the *A. frostiana,* which, according to *Edible and Poisonous Mushrooms of Canada,* published by Agriculture Canada, is 'said to be nonpoisonous but the danger of confusing it with *A. muscaria* is too great and it should be avoided at all times'. But I had a positive identification. There was no doubt.

My twelve specimens sitting there on the picnic table looked delicious. My mouth was watering. And so I fried them in butter and onions. Joan and the kids didn't want any so I ate all twelve. The first few were quite tasty but by the time I got to number 12 I knew something was wrong. In retrospect they caused an almost immediate chemical change in my body which affected my sense of taste. About ten seconds after I finished the twelfth one I realized I'd made a mistake, possibly the mistake of my life. My stomach started turning like a ferris wheel. But I didn't want the family to know I'd been poisoned. They would have been merciless, especially since I'd been trying to get them to share the mushrooms with me, telling them I was almost totally certain it was okay to eat them.

It was almost dark and we were going to the amphitheatre to see some nature films with all the other campers. But first I had to go to the washroom. 'I'll be right back,' I said as cheerfully as possible.

I puked for five minutes straight. It was horrible. I wrote on the wall, under Elwood Washington's jottings, 'Amanita frostiana deadly poisonous – The Voice of Experience.' Then I vomitted some more.

But there was something strange going on besides my illness. I knew I was sick, possibly fatally sick, but the curious chemical reaction had rendered me somehow insensitive to my own discomfort. Although I was vomiting fiercely I was at the same time rather delightfully inebriated. I felt as if I were floating above myself in an opium dream watching some fool down there being sick. The illness and the inebriation tended to cancel each other out. I wondered how inebriated I'd be if I weren't sick and how sick I'd be if I weren't inebriated.

'What took you so long?' said Joan.

I decided to go ahead with the big lie. 'Bit of constipation,' I said.

128

The Buddha Was No Dumb-Dumb

As we walked into the outdoor amphitheatre everything became blue. It was as if I were wearing blue sunglasses. That was the third effect. And then a fourth effect started: a feeling of extreme nervousness. My mind was racing like a Ferrari, thinking of everything except what was going on around me. And I began getting nauseous again. I began having doubts I would survive. But still I wouldn't let on.

We sat in the back row watching National Film Board films. The first was about Martians taking an Earth shot and finding our planet not to their liking. There was too much traffic for their taste. The whole film was a silly bore and a waste of money. I'd thought it all before.

The sky above the screen was more interesting. It was full of little silver, gold and purple clouds floating in the sunset. But I was having a hard time sitting still. Every atom in my body wanted to be elsewhere but I didn't know where. I envied the clouds.

There was a young couple sitting to my right. They had a little boy about three. A film about a bear came on the screen. 'Do you know why they call it a bear?' I said.

The kid didn't answer.

'Hey kid,' I said, vaguely aware that I was stoned on not-so-magic mushrooms. 'Do you know why they call that animal a bear?' The parents began laughing a little uncomfortably.

'Because he eats honey?' said the kid.

What a dumb answer, I thought. I suppose the kid was trying to be cute.

'No,' I said. 'Because he's not wearing any clothes. Haw Haw.'

What a dumb riddle, thought the kid. I suppose he's trying to be cute.

The main feature was something about the new underwater park off Tobermory. Fathom Five Provincial Park. When it started I knew I wouldn't be able to sit all the way through it. I was beginning to sweat.

'What's Fathom Five?' said Joan.

'It's a provincial park,' I snapped.

'Where is it?'

Was she kidding me? Was she just trying to annoy me? Did she know how uncomfortable I felt? Couldn't she hear my teeth chattering, see the sweat on my forehead? Why didn't I have the nerve simply to come clean and admit I'd made an honest mistake and poisoned myself? After all, even the Buddha died of mushroom poisoning and he was no dumb-dumb. I could tell her that just as I slipped into the big sleep.

'It's an underwater park off Tobermory,' I said curtly, hoping to convey the message I wasn't in the mood for further chit-chat.

'Oh, come on, Dave. Who would go to an underwater park?'

'Campers.'

'But you couldn't build campfires down there. And how would you keep your sleeping bags dry?'

The film started with shots of a winter storm off Georgian Bay, thirty-foot waves smashing into the naked cliffs of the Niagara Escarpment. It was making me sick.

I decided I had to come clean. 'Joan, I have to go and vomit. I might go to the car and lie down for a while or I might come right back. I don't know yet.' What a relief! I felt better already and I still hadn't puked.

Joan tried to look concerned but the big smile on her face displayed her true feelings. 'Oh are you sick, Dave?' she said. 'Something you ate maybe? Let's see now.' She was pretending to be dumb. 'What did you eat that none of us ate? I can't think of anything, can you?' My stomach was on fire. 'Oh of course. Those mushrooms! Maybe you've got a little itty-bitty touch of mushroom poisoning from those perfectly safe mushrooms you ate.'

I tried to make an elegant exit but I knew I wasn't going to

129
Joan Deduces the Cause of My Distress

succeed. I was only about thirty feet away from the back row when I resumed vomiting. It came with great heaving chokes and sobs that I'm sure could be heard all over the amphitheatre. It was a quiet part of the movie too. The symphonic soundtrack had gone dead for some dramatic reason. But no one came running to help me. They must have thought I was simply drunk.

When I got back to my feet my legs were like rubber. And again I didn't feel the slightest bit sick. The pressure was off my stomach and I felt totally rejuvenated, marvellous. I felt a total kinship with nature, a mystical identification with the entire universe. And everything was blue. Little blue squares floated in front of my eyes. I walked as if I were drunk but my mind was as clear as the Buddha's. Well, let's say I felt as if I'd finally tamed the ox and was riding it serenely back to the campsite.

Funny thing. As I write this months later my stomach is getting all churned up again.

---

130 Mushroom Poisoning

All night I slept shallowly, besieged by curious tension dreams about trying to scale the CN Tower, trying to scale a dozen fish for dinner, all that sort of thing. In the morning I felt worn out, as if I'd just written my bar examinations. My nerves were all swollen. With poison mushrooms the line becomes thick.

At the height of my distress however I knew I wasn't going to die. Because the symptoms were quite a bit different than the one really severe killer: *Amanita virosa*. Even a small amount of that mushroom can prove fatal. Here is what *Edible and Poisonous Mushrooms of Canada* has to say about *A. virosa* poisoning:

'The danger is increased by the fact that there is apparently no unpleasant taste and no symptoms are manifested until eight to twelve hours, or sometimes even longer, after the mushrooms are eaten. By this time the poison has been absorbed into the blood stream and the usual procedures such as pumping out the stomach are of no avail.... The general symptoms of this type of poisoning are severe abdominal pains, vomiting, cold sweats, diarrhea and excessive thirst. After persisting for some time the symptoms usually subside for a while and then recur more intensely; the liver is affected as well as the nervous system. There may be delirium, deep coma, and finally death. The patient suffers great pain.'

Anyway I dragged myself to the washroom just as the sun was beginning to sparkle in the dewdrops. And lo, overnight a poet had been born. Here's what he wrote, right next to Elwood Washington's complaint:

Not last night but the night before
Forty Robbers Came Adoor.
Went downstairs to let them
In Hit Me on the Head with
A Rolling Pin. Rolling pin was
made of brass. Turned me over
and hit my ass.

Question: What does this poem tell us about the poet?
Answer: He lives in a two-storey house and has masochistic fantasies.
Wrong: It could have been a three-storey house. And maybe it wasn't a fantasy. Maybe it really happened. Then again maybe it really was a fantasy and he lives in a one-storey house, or an apartment, or a room at the YMCA.

131
Alison Worries About Me

I ate a hearty breakfast so I guess I was all better. Joan and the kids weren't about to let me off the hook. They remembered that it could have been them just as easily.

I have an occasional problem with choking in the middle of the night. I wake up from the deepest level of sleep, sit bolt upright in bed and gasp loudly for air. Just as I've awakened everyone in the house and am about to turn blue I start breathing again. It's kind of frightening but it's been going on for eight years and I'm getting used to it. My friend Angela told her shrink about it and he told her to tell me not to worry, I wouldn't die.

'Did you choke last night, Daddy?' said Alison, slyly. She was learning from her mother. The exact tone of voice and everything. Perhaps Joan told her what to say.

'No', I said helplessly.

'You should eat poisonous mushrooms more often. Maybe they'll stop you from choking.'

132
The Retarded Kid from Sarnia

As we were cleaning up the breakfast dishes this retarded kid from Sarnia came by. He was about sixteen and was camping with his parents. He had a high forehead. He walked right into our campsite and began talking to us as if he'd known us all his life. He told us he didn't like these provincial parks as much as the private ones like the KOA (Kampers of America) campgrounds because there are no swimming pools in the provincial parks.

'Like to swim, do ya?' I said.

'Ya', he slobbered. I was out of matches so he went and got some from his brother.

Then he began complaining about the camp officers. He said they'd been speeding all over the place in their patrol cars earlier in the morning. He said somebody had a motorboat out on Cypress Lake, which is against the rules, and they were rushing around trying to get him out of there. He said he was worried someone would get run over by a patrol car.

'I'm more worried about duh speeding cop cars dan duh boat on duh lake', he said earnestly. You could tell he was quoting his parents. In fact his whole monologue seemed to have been lifted.

'How does your dad feel about that?' I said.

'He feels duh same way', he said.

After he left Joan turned to me. She'd found the kid delightful. 'You don't have to have a high IQ do you?' she said.

'Of course not', I said. 'He'd be nice to have around the house. He'd be worth his weight in laughs.'

I once knew a retarded fellow whom I used to see on the city bus occasionally. He would always sit at the front of the bus and do his imitations of radio announcers. He would give the morning news and hockey scores just perfectly, almost word for word.

One day he was giving the news as the bus headed down the Jolley Cut. He said a serious accident had just occurred at the foot of the Jolley Cut and motorists were advised to take another route downtown.

You guessed it. When the bus reached the bottom there had indeed been a serious accident. As the bus inched past, an ambulance pulled up. Everyone on the bus just stared at the fellow uneasily.

133
Young Fellows Flirting with Alison

So that was it. We decided our trip around Lake Huron was finished. We decided to drive home. Joan later said she wished we'd stayed a few more days at Cypress Lake Provincial Park but we didn't know at that time that we'd have to get rid of our van pretty soon and that would be our last camping trip. On any future trips around the Great Lakes we'd have to stay at motels.

We drove slowly, keeping just above the speed limit, all the way down the Bruce Peninsula to Owen Sound. The sky was incredibly blue and there were funny little cloud formations here and there that made you laugh out loud. You could see the road climbing up the next long low hill, and we knew we'd soon be climbing it too. We took turns guessing the distances to various points we could see way ahead of us. How many miles to the top of that hill?

How many miles before those funny clouds block the sun? And to think that in only a few months miles would be obsolete.

To be truthful I was fairly well bemushroomed, to use the term invented by the legendary mycologist Gordon Wasson. There seemed to be a lessening of the separation between me and the rest of the world, between me and the divinity within us. We were all of the same dimension, the same inner pigment. Everything was moving slowly and peacefully as we stopped here and there for soft drinks and just to look at things. I'd eaten the poison mushrooms but my state was picked up by the others. The moment sort of expanded. A single moment seemed to go on forever.

At one point a car with the letters EYS on its licence passed us on the road. I thought it would be nice to have a licence number with the letters EYE. And a few minutes later, so help me, we were passed by a car with the letters EYE on its licence.

We had lunch in Wiarton. The restaurant was decorated with a series of framed colour photos of a huge iceberg off Newfoundland. It was interesting. We'd heard that Stompin' Tom Connors had a summer home in the Wiarton area but the restaurant owner didn't know anything about it.

Some young fellows about fourteen or fifteen at the next table were flirting with Alison. In fact they came in just to get a better look at her. She's getting to look a little like Anne Murray. Jenny's more the Jane Fonda type.

And that's about the way this book ends. When we got home our mileage was 61013.6 which meant we'd gone 1248.4 on this trip as compared with 800 miles exactly on the Lake Erie trip.

I see too I'm winding up on manuscript page 252. Funny coincidence. *A Trip around Lake Erie* had 252 manuscript pages too. But that one had 142 chapters as compared with Lake Huron's 133.

Don't know where we're going next. Maybe Lake Superior. Maybe Lake Michigan. Maybe Lake Ontario. Maybe nowhere.

Typeset in Century Schoolbook and Helvetica Black
Printed in Canada at The Coach House Press
401 (rear) Huron Street, Toronto, Canada M5S 2G5

Photography: Montecolour
Text Design: Glenn Goluska